BORN GREAT

How to be who you are, have what you want, and change the world

Emily Gowor

Born Great: How to be who you are, have what you want, and change the world
© Emily Gowor 2019

www.emilygowor.com

The moral rights of Emily Gowor to be identified as the author of this work have been asserted in accordance with the Copyright Act 1968.

First published in Australia 2019 by Gowor International Publishing.

ISBN 978-0-6483574-6-9

Any opinions expressed in this work are exclusively those of the author and are not necessarily the views held or endorsed by Gowor International Publishing.

All rights reserved. No part of this publication may be reproduced or transmitted by any means, electronic, photocopying, or otherwise, without prior written permission of the author.

Disclaimer

All the information, techniques, skills, and concepts contained within this publication are of the nature of general comment only and are not in any way recommended as individual advice. The intent is to offer a variety of information to provide a wider range of choices now and in the future, recognising that we all have widely diverse circumstances and viewpoints. Should any reader choose to make use of the information herein, this is their decision, and the author and publisher(s) do not assume any responsibilities whatsoever under any conditions or circumstances. The author does not take responsibility for the business, financial, personal, or other success, results, or fulfilment upon the readers' decision to use this information. It is recommended that the reader obtain their own independent advice.

Dedicated to Laraib Malik for inspiring me to write this book and for reminding me of the importance of my soul's calling.

Foreword

I first met Emily when she was just 19 years old and attended my weekend signature program, *The Breakthrough Experience*®. She was experiencing depression and suicidal thoughts and questioning whether her life was worth living.

That weekend, Emily saw a glimpse of the inherent yet dormant greatness inside her, and in the decade that followed, I watched Emily transform her life by pursuing what is inside her heart: her love of writing. Her mission to inspire people to live an extraordinary life has seen both her presence and her work touch the lives of what is now thousands of people around the world.

After more than four and a half decades of working with human behaviour in my career, I am certain that every individual has far greater potential than many may realise, and that it is in the pursuit of what we feel the most inspired to do that we discover the truth of our own magnificence.

Emily and her story are living proof of this. She is far more mature in her wisdom than she is in her years, and I know she will inspire you through this book and show you that your life, too, can be deeply meaningful.

Emily's new book will now inspire you to give yourself permission to do something extraordinary on planet Earth.

Dr John Demartini
International best-selling author of *The Values Factor*

Preface

When I first started writing *Born Great*, I had no idea just how significant the journey ahead would be. I also didn't foresee how much the book would evolve from the day I began writing it to the day it was published, or how much I would grow along with it.

I wasn't prepared for how deep it would take me into my innermost thoughts and feelings or how much patience and persistence it would require for me to complete it. I was blissfully unaware of the many ways in which it would challenge me to deepen my belief that I, too, was 'born great', just as the title of this book states.

Anyone who has met me knows that my mission is to write and inspire people. When I'm not hands-on with this mission, I am thinking or dreaming about it. This book is the manifestation of my calling to help humanity reach for greater lives. It is my PhD on living your dreams and my guide to creating a meaningful life. Within it, I will share all the inspiration I can offer to make sure that your time on Earth is nothing short of extraordinary.

To say that it has required enormous effort to share my message with you in this book is an understatement. I shed tears for it, struggled with it, made sacrifices for it, and flew across the country and the world to write it for you. There were times when I considered giving up on it, but I couldn't; the vision I saw of how it could impact your life was far too alluring and important to walk away from. In fact, ever since the idea first appeared in my mind as three words - vision, wealth, and work - I knew that this book was destined to be written.

And so, the only thing left to do was to continue through every twist and turn until it reached this moment, today, where you hold it firmly in your hands. Having now fulfilled my next ambition as an author, I can say without question that every single hour spent placing words where they belong and every moment where I pushed myself, both as a writer and as a woman, has been worth it.

To me, *Born Great* is not just a book; it is an expression of my purpose. My greatest wish and highest hope while writing it was that it will help you to find and fulfil your own purpose, too. I hope that it comes to be one of the most moving books you read on the topic of connecting with your calling and making your difference to the human race.

You will find my heart in these pages as well as the deepest wisdom I have gained on how to make your life one that is truly worth living. As you embark on the journey of reading this book, it is my heartfelt wish that I have achieved my mission and that, by the time you turn the last page, you will know what your heart yearns to do and have the courage to pursue it without hesitation, wherever it may take you.

May each page help you to see greater possibilities for yourself so that you can experience what I believe is the most inspiring way to live and work: from your soul. May you find the answers you have been seeking about your purpose, and thus the greater purpose of your life. And may you catch a lasting glimpse of how magnificent you are so that you never give up on the journey of fulfilling the inspiring destiny you were born for.

Table of Contents

Foreword vii
Preface ix
Introduction 1

Part 1: Vision 7
   1: Live Your Life on Purpose 8
   2: The Courage to Be Yourself 25
   3: Unleash Your Greatness 42
   4: Your Destiny Is Calling 59

Part 2: Wealth 77
   5: Great Riches Await You 78
   6: You Are Worthy of Wealth 95
   7: Find Your Financial Power 110
   8: Claim Your Fortunes 126

Part 3: Work 143
   9: Use Your Work to Change the World 144
   10: Grow the Career of Your Dreams 159
   11: You Can Fly to Great Heights 175
   12: The World Is Waiting for Your Greatness 192

Conclusion 209
You Were Born Great 214
Acknowledgements 216
About The Author 218

Introduction

"There is no greater gift you can give or receive than to honour your calling. It's why you were born. And how you become most truly alive."

Oprah Winfrey

It is no secret that the majority of the human race feel lost and unfulfilled. While there are many people who have found their path of purpose and shot up to the top of their field, making waves in the world as they go, there are still billions of people stumbling around in the dark. Billions of people who are wondering what the point of being alive is and questioning whether their life has real meaning in the grand scheme of it all.

Billions of people who dread going to work in the morning and who haven't yet realised that they, too, could thrive on Earth. Billions of people who are keeping their dreams locked up inside their heart, blindly unaware of just how extraordinary they truly are. Billions of people who have not yet realised that they were born great.

I was one of these people. As I will share early on in the book, I was so depressed at the young age of 19 that I nearly ended my life. I felt small and insignificant, as if I didn't matter. Today, I am immensely grateful that I chose to live, as I have now spent more than ten years living in pursuit of my purpose and experiencing the beauty and magic of the world.

All that has happened between the critical moment, where I came close to giving up completely, and this critical moment today, where I am reaching out to you through these words, has formed the essential foundation of this book. In fact, it is the entire reason I wrote it for you.

See, I know that deep down on the inside, you don't want to live a mediocre life; you want to live an extraordinary one. I know that you don't want to settle for an empty existence; you want to live in pursuit of greater possibilities. And, I know that you don't want to accept the career, relationships, and financial status that are dealt to you along the way. You want to live your life by design, not by default. To do this, you must realise that you are capable of far greater things than you have ever dreamed could be possible for you.

For many people, this is easier said than done. In fact, the moment you read those words, you probably pictured a list in your mind of all the reasons you think you don't have greatness within you. It's likely that you started this list a long time ago, perhaps as early as childhood, and it is still with you today. But, regardless of what is on that list or what anyone has said to or about you in the past, I'm here to tell you that the seed of greatness is within you, and the entire purpose of your life's journey is to discover that greatness and share it.

That voice in your head that says you are not tall, strong, rich, beautiful, or bold enough to fulfil your dream is your insecurities speaking, not your soul. It is a lie, and far from the truth about who you are. You were born whole and complete and made of the right stuff. That is true of every single human being, no exceptions. So, if you have spent your whole life telling yourself that you don't deserve to be, do, and have

Introduction

what you want, then it is time to reconsider, because you are thinking far too little of yourself.

Each human being expresses greatness differently, from dancers and magicians to high-flying company leaders and devoted parents. While some of us may express it more than others, the fire of potential burns equally within all of us. No matter what is happening right now or what happened yesterday, that flame never goes out. You might feel weighed down by adversity or confused about what to do next as you sit there reading this, but you were not born without that spark of purpose, and my mission is to help it burn brighter than ever.

Regardless of whether we are meeting for the very first time or if we have known each other for years, I believe that I am here to help you find your path and place in the world, and through that, uncover the deep meaning of your life. I am here to remind you of the calling that lives within you, and to inspire your courage to follow it against all logic, outside opinion, and any self-doubt that might arise along the way. For you to fulfil your potential is what I want the most for you, and I will be there on every page of this book encouraging you to reach out and take it.

This book has been written in three parts. In Part 1: Vision, we will delve into your purpose, destiny, and anything that stands between you today and the life that you would love to live. In Part 2: Wealth, we will explore your relationship with money so that you can be paid for your gift and experience all that life has to offer. In the third and final part of the book, Part 3: Work, I will support you to grow the career of your dreams while making a difference in the lives of people all over the world.

My intention, as we take this journey together, is that your mind will be filled with ideas on how to close the gap between your work and your purpose, between your work and your wealth, and between where you are and where you want to be. It is to have you realise just how worthy you are of an extraordinary life and to take you closer to the heartfelt vision you see for your future. It is to help you wake up each morning feeling inspired by the next 24 hours of your time here on Earth; by where you will go, what you will do, and who you will spend it with.

It is to remind you that we only experience each day once, so we'd best make the most of every moment by discovering what lights us up from within and going after it. It is to help you believe to your core that who you are has great significance and value. And, above all, it is to help you be who you are, have what you want, and change the world.

A natural progression occurs in the journey of creating a life that inspires us. First, our longing for fulfilment leads us to connect with our purpose, to find and do what we love. Then, we discover a desire to earn an income from our purpose so that we can spend our life doing work that has deep meaning to us. And finally, as we share our gifts with the world, we experience a yearning to make our ultimate contribution to humanity.

I believe that this journey is the most rewarding one a human being can take, as it is on this journey that we find out who we truly are, share our gifts, and leave an inspiring legacy in our wake. This is precisely why it is anything but selfish to pursue your dream, because what starts out as a tiny spark of inspiration can soon light up the lives of those around you.

The world is overflowing with people who haven't managed to establish a thriving career doing what they love and changing the world in the process. Perhaps the reason for this is because they haven't realised how valuable they are to humanity. Perhaps they don't feel worthy or capable of fulfilling their heartfelt desires. Or, perhaps they have no idea just how rewarding their life could and would be if they surrendered their fears and gave their dream their all.

This saddens me, as so many people take their gifts to the grave with them; gifts that could have changed the future for one person, maybe thousands, or even a million people. If only we realised just how needed we are and how powerful what we have inside us is, we would surely stop standing in our own way and begin living boldly in pursuit of our purpose instead.

If you want to break out of the mould and live a life of deep meaning, this book is for you. If you are ready to follow and fulfil your calling, these pages will encourage you to do just that. And, if you are prepared to do whatever it takes to be true to yourself and make your mark on the world, then what I will share will prepare you for the journey. Welcome home.

When you see an inspiring vision for your future and devote yourself to creating it, what will happen next will be nothing short of extraordinary. In fact, I can barely begin to describe just how fulfilling your life is about to become as you discover and express the greatness within you. However, what I can say to you is that it will change beyond recognition, and it all starts by deciding what you would love to do in the time that you have been given and devoting yourself to a life lived on purpose.

PART 1
VISION

1

Live Your Life on Purpose

"It is only when we truly know and understand that we have a limited time on Earth - and that we have no way of knowing when our time is up - that we will begin to live each day to the fullest, as if it was the only one we had."

Elisabeth Kubler-Ross

Don't you want to live a life that matters? One where you express all that you are and do all that you can? One where you leave nothing unsaid and no dream unfulfilled? One at the end of which you can say, with a hand on your heart, that you lived with purpose? That is the commitment I want to invite you to make today: that you will do whatever it takes to create that life for yourself.

If you haven't already begun to reflect on the deeper meaning of being alive, I know that you will eventually start to wonder. Someday - maybe today, maybe tomorrow, or maybe in ten years from now - you will take a step back, evaluate the purpose of your life, and ask yourself, "What is it all for?" My hope is that you will choose to live, love, and work in such a way that, at the end of your years, the answer to this question will be so profound, so beautiful, and so inspiring that tears will roll down your cheeks.

We have an innate need as human beings to have a sense of direction for the future and a purpose to fulfil. It is hard-wired into us, at the core of our design, to seek more; to conquer new terrains, see incredible sights from mountaintops, and discover all that we are made of. We each have the calling for a greater future within us, and it is what we are all capable of.

The more we nurture this desire to expand and explore, the more alive, aligned, and inspired we feel. A meaningless and monotonous life becomes a thing of the past, and we start to thrive, not just survive. It is then and there that we rise up, unfold our destiny, and experience the richest rewards that being alive has to offer.

From Depression to Inspiration

I lay on the floor one night, aged 19. The only thought that kept running through my mind was, 'I don't care if my heart ever beats again.' I had dropped out of university a year earlier after discovering that a path of academia wasn't my calling. My head and heart were pulling me in two different directions, and I couldn't ignore my heart anymore. After putting my degree in Sociology and Philosophy on hold, I spent the next eight months feeling deeply depressed.

I no longer cared about socialising or meeting new people, studying didn't interest me, and the thought of being with a partner felt pointless. I had lost all motivation to do anything that would be considered 'normal'. Even the relationships I had with my loved ones began to fade away into the background. My world had come to a standstill; I had fallen through the cracks between school and life.

A handful of people were nudging me to get a job as a friend was paying my rent and bills at the time, but I was too consumed by my pain to look for work. I barely wanted to get up in the morning, let alone get dressed, go to an office, and put on a face pretending I was fine when I was drowning on the inside. Life felt pointless, because I hadn't connected with what the point of my life was yet. The days felt like a blur. It didn't seem to matter what happened, who I saw, or what I did. I felt empty inside.

I was searching for answers, and I was hurting. I felt insignificant and alone, lost in a sea of billions of people. Why did I matter? Who cared if I lived or died? I couldn't see that I had anything to offer people let alone that I had a greater destiny to fulfil on Earth. I felt like I had hit a dead-end, and I didn't know what to do or where to turn next. But then one night, in the middle of the year, it changed dramatically and permanently.

I had reached rock bottom, and a deep sense of hopelessness had washed over me. So, while I was driving my car from the south-west suburbs into the city of Brisbane, I contemplated ending my life. I was driving at 80kmph on the freeway when I eyed the concrete barrier that separated the lanes of traffic. I thought to myself, 'What if I just write myself off, right here and now? The pain will end, and I won't have to do this anymore.'

A few seconds later, I turned the steering wheel to the right and steered the car towards the concrete barrier… and then I turned it back. My heart was beating fast inside my chest. I took a deep breath and tried to summon my courage to do it - to wipe my presence off the planet forever - and turned the car to face the barrier a second time… and then I turned it back again.

I couldn't do it. Aside from my survival instinct kicking in and desperately trying to save me from my own demise, something had stirred deep within me: I knew that it wasn't my time to die, and that this wasn't how I was meant to go. I felt frustrated, as though I'd failed myself by not having the courage to go through with it and relieve myself of the emotional struggle that had been consuming me for months. But, despite this, coming so close to the edge of my own existence had woken something up in me - call it my heart, my soul, or a glimpse of my destiny - and I knew that what I was feeling inside was right. My life wasn't over yet… far from it.

I drove home, parked on the street, and walked through the front door of my apartment, feeling numb. I dropped my keys onto the kitchen bench and stood there for a moment before laying down on a mattress on the lounge-room floor. I lay there for twelve long hours. I didn't move, I didn't eat, I didn't go to the bathroom, and I didn't speak to anyone. I was 19, smart, and big-hearted, and yet I felt like I didn't have anything to live for. But even in that moment when I had been stripped bare and I was drowning in my sorrow, there was a part of me that knew that my life didn't have to be this way.

Deep inside my heart, I didn't believe that we are put here on Earth to suffer. I believed that we are born with a purpose as well as the ability to thrive in the pursuit of it. I knew that I wasn't as insignificant as I thought I was and thinking that my life had no meaning was a lie I'd been believing for years. And, even though I thought it didn't matter if my heart ever beat again, I knew that, actually, my heart beating was the most important thing of all. It mattered greatly that I lived.

So, in that moment, I decided that I would do whatever it took to create an extraordinary life for myself and help other people to do the same. I made this decision for two reasons: the first was that giving up was simply not an option anymore. The second was that I yearned to experience something magnificent, inspiring, and meaningful while alive.

I didn't really want my life to end. In fact, the truth was the opposite. I wanted to start living fully, with everything that I had and everything that I was. I wanted to be exactly who I was born to be; an inspirational writer who showed people the beauty around them and within them. I wanted to travel to great places, stand on tall mountains, feel the rain on my skin, and express what was inside my heart.

During my rock bottom moment, I saw a picture in my mind of how I wanted my future to be and, as it turned out, that vision saved me. It pulled me back from the brink of my own extinction and pointed me in the direction I wanted to go. It was the beginning of a whole new pathway towards the life I couldn't wait to live.

I knew that fulfilling my dream would require relentless devotion. I knew that it would require an enormous amount of personal healing and work to make it happen. I also knew that it would not be the easiest thing I had ever done. But I didn't care - I wanted in - and it was in that moment as I lay on the floor feeling more alone and depressed than ever that I made the decision to give my dream everything I had.

That night was a critical turning point in my journey. I finally let the past be the past. I let go of who I thought I should be and accepted myself for who I was. I found the determination I needed to pick myself up and keep going. And, from that moment forwards, I became committed to the pursuit and fulfilment of what mattered the most to me: my heartfelt mission to inspire people.

The journey to transform my life didn't happen overnight, but it did happen. I began working on myself. I knew I had to start by finding out who I was and build from there. So, I spent three hours a day doing self-development for more than a year. I filled several journals as I explored my innermost thoughts and feelings, questioning every voice in my head that said I couldn't do what I dreamed of doing.

Gradually, through my dedication to my emotional healing, my life began to feel less like a bottomless pit of meaninglessness. I began to feel that I deserved to thrive and that I was worthy of unconditional love, great achievement, and deep fulfilment, just the way I was. I rediscovered my love of writing, which I had coincidentally stopped doing during the months I experienced depression, and I began networking at business events in my city. Within a few short months, my career as a professional writer had begun - and the rest is history.

Pursuing my dream led me to great places, including travelling the globe writing a multiple award-winning blog, working with influential leaders, and speaking on stages in Australia and abroad. I launched international projects, won young entrepreneur awards, and became a published author for the first time when I was just 23 years old. The depression that had previously consumed me soon gave way and inspiration took its place. I was well on my way to living the life I'd imagined.

Facing depression revealed what truly mattered to me. I realised that I did know what I wanted to do, and although I couldn't see every step of the road to get there, I could see where I wanted to go, which in and of itself was life-changing. Had I not come face-to-face with my mortality as a teenager, I may never have discovered many of the things that fill my days with magic today.

The moral of my story is in the immense power that a heartfelt dream has to change your life forever, if you have the courage to acknowledge and follow it. But for this to happen, you must first decide that, like me, you are going to do whatever it takes to make your time on Earth extraordinary. I believe to my core that this is not only what you deserve, but that it is what you were born for - so, choose.

Choose to connect deeply with your calling and pursue it down every path it beckons you to go. Choose to let a brighter future guide you in every decision you make and how you live each day. And above all, choose that you will take this life and make it what you dream of, no matter what you might face along the way, because a whole new life is possible for you, too.

The Spark of an Extraordinary Future

No matter where you are today, you can create a deeply meaningful future for yourself. You can go from the bottom to the top, from lost to found, and from struggling to flourishing. The journey to do exactly that begins in the moment that you decide you won't settle for an empty existence. It begins in the moment that you decide you want to thrive in every way imaginable, and that you want every single day that you are alive to be part of a beautiful story unfolding.

A conscious connection to your purpose is the starting point of that life. Simply put, this means having a deep sense of what you love to do; what you were born to do. You might refer to it as your calling, your destiny, or the higher plan for your life. Regardless of the name you give it, this awareness of your purpose is the source of the deep fulfilment that we yearn for as well as the foundation upon which an inspiring future can be built.

I first discovered my purpose as a writer at age 14. High school was a challenging experience as I was socially ostracised and sometimes bullied. One Friday night, after a particularly rough week, I found myself sitting alone in front of the family computer, feeling dejected. It seemed that no one understood what I was going through, not even my parents, and it felt as though I was on my own in the world.

Suddenly, something washed over me. I opened up a word document on the computer and began typing. In a matter of minutes, I had written a poem onto the screen in front of me. The poem expressed how I felt, sharing the depth of my emotions. As I completed the poem, I felt calm and present. It had healed me, and although I didn't know it at the time, I had found my calling: to write.

I wrote behind closed doors, during lunch breaks at school, and late at night when everyone was sleeping. That year alone, I produced 170 poems as well as a series of abstract prose, and I haven't stopped putting pen to page since. I didn't write because it looked cool or because someone told me I should; I wrote because everything made sense when I did. When life felt confusing, I used the page as an outlet for my feelings and as a way to sort through my thoughts.

I wasn't thinking about how I could help people or change the world with my words at the time, nor was I thinking about how much money I could make doing it. I just knew that I loved to write and that when I wrote, I felt alive. Whenever I touched my fingertips to the keyboard, I knew who I was and what I wanted to spend my life doing.

Over the years, my writing evolved from pieces that revealed my teenage angst, which often gave my teachers a cause for concern, into uplifting self-help content. That same, insatiable urge to write followed me all the way through high school and into adulthood. It not only shaped the career path I chose and the achievements that followed, but it also brought deep meaning to my entire life. In many ways, it was also the reason I overcame my depression at age 19.

It is because of the heart-opening transformation discovering my calling has brought to me that, today, I am convinced that connecting with your purpose is the most powerful thing you can do if you are serious about living a life at the end of which, you know that you have explored all that is truly possible for you.

Knowing why we are here is the difference between an empty life and a full one, between someone who never makes it big and someone who rises to the top, and between an average day and a rewarding one. This is why taking the time to discover your purpose matters greatly.

How will you know that you have found your purpose? There will be no question about it. You will feel it. The hairs will stand up on your arms and legs. Goosebumps will ripple across your body. Your heart will open. You will feel connected to the world around you and within you. Tears of inspiration will fill your eyes or even flow freely down your face.

You will become determined, persistent, innovative, ambitious, and moved by something far beyond you. You will know where you are going and exactly what it is that makes you so special, unique, and extraordinary. Many of the questions that you have been asking about what your future holds will be answered.

Your purpose isn't a complex riddle to solve; it's simple. As simple as writing is for me, as business-building is for entrepreneurs, as weight-lifting is for performance coaches, as dancing is for dancers, as painting is for painters, and as singing is for singers. It is what you feel called to do and why you have life force flowing through you in this very moment; so that you can connect with and pursue your purpose to the very end.

If you have no idea where to start in connecting with your purpose, begin by eliminating what it's not. For example, I discovered during high school that while I had the potential to excel at mathematics and was once an A-grade student, solving problems with numbers didn't interest me. This firmly ruled out careers in the finance industry as well as any other industry that involved extensive mathematics.

I also knew that I felt like a fish out of water when playing sport. This took several other career paths off the table, including those related to the study and treatment of the human body. I began to focus on subjects that involved the English language, letting go of other pursuits until it became evident to me that I loved to write, and that my topic was self-development.

Every time you surrender a purpose that you know isn't yours, you will move closer to the one that is, until one day it is staring you in the face. When that happens, you will be able to look out at the world around you with clarity on what your place within it is. You will know what you are here to do, and you will no longer be able to deny who you truly are.

Maybe you will have to give up ideas about who you think you are supposed to be in order to connect with your purpose. But if you spend your life thinking that you are supposed to work in a job when, in your heart, you know you were born to be an entrepreneur, or invest your time studying to be a doctor when deep inside you want to dance, your spirit will die before your body does. You need your purpose and it needs you: you were made for each other. Thus, the courage to let go of what you are not called to do is worth it. Remember, this is your life we are talking about, and it matters greatly that you are ignited from within every day.

In an interview, Italian sculptor Michelangelo was asked how he carved the Statue of David. His response was profound. He said, "I simply removed everything that was not David." It is in having the courage to admit and then surrender what does not move you, that you will not only discover what your future holds but start to believe that your presence matters.

As you pursue your true purpose, you will begin to comprehend the meaning and value of your life, both to you and to the world around you. You will realise that you were born with a unique destiny and the potential to fulfil it, and that you are worthy of success, just the way you are.

So, understand that there is nothing wrong with you if what you want to devote your life to is different to what your family, friends, and colleagues do. We are each an original design and it is precisely our uniqueness that makes us so extraordinary. It does not mean that you are a failure if you find academia difficult, and it does not make you inferior if your family are athletic while you trip over your feet when a ball is kicked your way. You just haven't stumbled upon the purpose that is undeniably yours yet.

You might know people who are living an amazing life doing what they love, and you may be wondering if you have a purpose that is as inspiring and powerful as theirs. But trust me when I say that it is not missing from you. In fact, believing that you have no real purpose or value is like believing that the flowers need no sunshine. You were born with it and born because of it, and even if you can't see it, it's there. Every single step of your journey so far has been trying to reveal it to you; life has been dropping hints and leaving clues, hoping that today is the day you awaken to the inspiring reason for your existence on planet Earth.

So, pay close attention to the times when you feel the most alive. They are the trail to your treasure, and when you find that treasure, all other paths will fade away. Don't undervalue it, deny it, ignore it, repress it, or push it to the side. Take it firmly in both hands and cherish it, because you have found something that few human beings find: the role you were born to play on the stage of life.

Sometimes we look to the world around us to answer the existential question about why we were born and thus, what the purpose of our life is. But here's the thing: no one can tell you what your purpose is. It's something that only your heart and soul knows. Therefore, you must look deep within you to connect with it, as that is the only way that you will know that you have found it. It is only by feeling it that you will know this purpose is YOURS.

There will be no mistaking whether you have found your path of destiny. You either feel inspired to pursue it or you don't. It either moves you or it doesn't. You're either intrigued by it or not. You either can't wait to do it or you couldn't care less if you do it at all. If you hear yourself thinking or saying, "I just want to (x)," or "I wish I could spend all my time doing (y)," then you're on the right track. If it comes to you naturally, you might be onto something. And if thoughts of doing it consume your mind every single day, then you know that you have found it. You have discovered what lights you up and solved the mystery about what you are here on Earth to do.

Whatever it takes to connect with your heartfelt purpose, it's worth the journey, because it truly is the difference between the life that you are living today and the one that you dream of. It is the difference between feeling alive or empty on the inside, between wandering aimlessly through life and being fired up from within, and between life being an endless struggle and the greatest adventure that you ever take.

When you connect with your purpose, it will become your guiding light and your true north. You will lose and find yourself in pursuit of it. And, it will become the ultimate avenue for self-discovery and self-expression, as well as the key to your success.

It doesn't matter if it takes you two days, two months, two years, or even two decades to find it. It just matters greatly that you find it. It will inspire you endlessly and give you every reason to not only live, but live fully. So, seek the defining moment where you meet your purpose and it meets you because, when that moment happens, you will find yourself standing at the start of a radically different life.

Make Your Purpose the Centrepiece of Your Life

Once you have connected with your purpose, there is just one thing left to do: make it the centrepiece of your life. How do you do this? First, spend time on it every day, whether that is practising music, developing ideas for a global business, learning about investing, or training your body for peak performance. Make it a priority by scheduling it into your calendar. Then, plan your entire future around it.

Which career path will allow you to fulfil it? What mission would you love to devote yourself to? What dream is worth working for? What great adventures would you love to have that will make each day of your time here a gift? What impact would you love to have in the world? Where would you love to live, visit, work, and travel? Who would you love to spend time with? What would you love to achieve? Do? Feel? See? Experience?

The clearer you are on what a life centred around your purpose looks like, the quicker you can create it. You can't move from where you are to where you want to be if you don't know where you are going, and if where you are going doesn't excite you, you won't apply yourself to get there. But once you are clear on where you are heading and you start moving towards it, your journey will soon become an amazing adventure of transforming your dream into a reality.

After experiencing depression at age 19, I began working on the task at hand: giving myself the extraordinary life I had vowed to myself I would create. I knew that, in order to do this, I would need to know what that involved, otherwise I would have no chance of fulfilling it. So, I completed a simple and profound exercise.

I took a piece of paper and a pen and wrote down a list of all the things that inspired me. I filled the page with things like 'writing', 'travel', 'deep conversation', 'city lights', and 'music'. I figured it was a logical exercise. After all, if I wanted to live an inspiring life, it made sense to fill my life with what inspired me - and that's exactly what I did.

Over the two to three years that followed, I made a conscious effort to do and experience as many things from my list as possible, as often as possible. As I did this, I not only began to feel alive and inspired each day, but I also built the foundation for my entire career. By doing what I loved, I started influencing the lives of others and people began asking me how I had created the life I was living. They wanted to fulfil their dreams, too.

By immersing myself in and surrounding myself with people, places, and activities that touched, moved, and inspired me, I had begun to touch, move, and inspire those around me. Likewise, writing your own list today may be the key to the life and career you would love tomorrow, as well as the difference you dream of making.

Most people live by default. They accept the circumstances, jobs, relationships, and opportunities that cross their path and don't dare dream for more. I say, be courageous enough to live by design instead, and create a life where each moment enriches your existence on Earth. Even if no one in your family has done it before and even if it seems strange to your friends, stop at nothing to give yourself that life.

Many years ago, I facilitated on a personal development program where the participants were asked to write down what they wanted in the future. A woman in her sixties approached me for assistance. "So, you're saying that I just write down what I want?" she asked me. My heart broke as I realised that no one had ever told her that she could decide how she wanted her life to be.

For six decades, she had been doing what other people expected of her without considering that perhaps she had dreams and aspirations, too. As I supported her to decide how she wanted to spend her remaining years, my resolve to inspire people to reach for more strengthened ten-fold.

Our societal and education systems don't necessarily encourage us to find out who we are and what our unique purpose is. But, if you ignore your calling, you will miss out on thousands of incredible experiences where you connect heart-to-heart with people, see sights so beautiful they bring tears to your eyes, and feel inspired to your core. And, in my humble opinion, you will miss out on what I have come to believe being alive is all about: the spiritual satiation of fulfilling your soul's purpose.

You already have a picture inside your mind of the life you want for yourself - of what you see yourself doing and of what you dream you can become - and your purpose is central to that picture. It may be buried underneath the reasons you think you can't have what you want or hidden behind the fear of whether what you desire is possible, but it is there. So, find the courage to reveal it to yourself because that picture is the map that you need to navigate your way to an enriching future.

It doesn't matter where you are, how old you are, or how far away you might appear to be from that picture right now. It's irrelevant. That's not what defines your destiny. I started my journey with $2.13 in my bank account, no job, no business skills, no brand, and no plan. I just had a vision for my future, and I was determined to make it happen.

So, begin to move in the direction of your dream. Start from where you are today and build towards where you want to go. Even if the changes that you make to align your future with your purpose are small to begin with, they will transform your life from the inside out. A baby step is still a step forwards, and it is what you do daily that builds your destiny.

Focus on closing the gap between what you do and what you love to do, between what you love to do and what you are paid to do, and between what you are paid to do and what you feel you were born to do. And lastly, don't ever give up on yourself, because everything you have ever dreamed of is hidden behind the door to which your purpose is the key.

Deep inside us, we know that discovering and pursuing our purpose is the key to fulfilment in every area, from professional accomplishments to personal relationships, and you will get so much more out of life if you decide to embark on the journey consciously. That is, if you choose to listen to and follow the niggling feeling within you that tells you there is far more to life (and far more to you) than what you have experienced up until this moment.

Remember: you exist for an important reason, and if you walk forwards believing this, even in the darkest of moments, you won't fail. You can't fail. On the contrary, it will be just a matter of time before you are thriving in ways that you didn't know were possible for you. The fact that you are still here tells me that you are not done, and it doesn't matter how far you've already come, you have just begun. So, make your purpose the main focus of your future and you will soon be waking up every day to a deeply meaningful life; a life lived on purpose.

*****

Maybe you'll have to travel the world, see great places, and take an 'eat, pray, love' journey to discover what you and your life are all about. Then again, maybe you won't. Maybe it's in your own backyard. Maybe you'll stumble across it when you walk down the street tomorrow. Maybe it will come to you in your next meditation, or maybe you'll connect with it during a relationship break-up or on the day you are fired from your job. Or maybe you will wake up tomorrow morning knowing what it is.

But regardless of what journey you go on to find it, it is there waiting to be discovered; it is what you and your life are all about.

Your purpose. Your thing. Your calling. What moves you from within, like the music moves the dancer. When you stumble across it, it will be unmistakable; an unforgettable moment. When that moment happens, never again will there be a reason to doubt its presence or feel that you don't belong in this world… because you will be home.

2

The Courage to Be Yourself

"To be yourself in a world that is constantly trying to make you something else is the greatest accomplishment."

Ralph Waldo Emerson

How far you go in life rests largely on how deep your courage to be yourself is, no matter what people around you might say. We are often so concerned about other's opinions of us that we hold back from our dream or give up on it altogether. We waste precious time that could otherwise be spent on what matters most - pursuing our purpose - and in doing so, we miss out on the extraordinary life that is possible for us.

But here's the thing: no one makes an impact by trying to fit in and following the norm. It is in breaking the mould, not in trying to change parts of ourselves to fit in, that we discover that there is no one else like us and that this is a magnificent thing. And so, to express your greatness, to fly, to rise to the top, you must be willing to stand out by being the one-of-a-kind design that you were born to be.

If we follow the crowd and hold back from being who we are in an attempt to belong, we will live our entire life in hiding. But, if you cherish your originality and all that makes you different instead, you will experience a depth of meaning during your time on Earth that will make you wonder why you waited so long to be faithful to what your soul yearns to do.

You Are Perfection Made Manifest

I imagine that, as you sit there reading this, you feel that there is something wrong with you or that, on some level, you aren't enough. I imagine that you have been keeping a mental list of the ways you think you should change or improve parts of yourself. And, I imagine that you are keeping a scorecard in your mind of what you think you have succeeded or failed at, and that you tend to focus on the failures rather than on your accomplishments. I get it. I do it, too.

But, let me ask you this: why do you think that you aren't magnificent in your very design? And, where does the notion that you, in any way, need altering? Is it because of something that someone said to or about you? Because you were bullied as a child? Because you dropped out of school before completing your senior year?

Perhaps your partner cheated on you in your last relationship or you lost a large sum of money. Or maybe your career or business hasn't taken off yet. Regardless of the reason, if you are going to discover just how extraordinary you truly are, then it is time to consider changing how you see yourself and embrace the truth that you are perfect to the core.

See, human beings tend to presume that they are not worthy. We add together all the moments from the past when we were rejected, bullied, criticised, left out, or judged and draw a conclusion that there is something wrong with us. We falsely assume that if we were worthy, then we wouldn't experience challenges in life, when this is an unavoidable part of being human.

This assumption that we are somehow lesser causes us to settle for less than what we long for and, in many cases, we never find the courage to live the way our heart desires. We start to seek approval from people, even those who we don't know personally or, worse, from people who are living smaller lives than the one we dream of.

Our greatness remains hidden from ourselves and the world for as long as we believe that we are somehow flawed. But when we begin to see ourselves clearly, as we actually are and not as we think we are, our hearts open, our vision for the future becomes clear, and our life starts to take off.

The reason that you think you aren't perfect the way you are is because you keep taking yourself at face value. Yes, you are being shallow with yourself. You keep measuring your results against those of others around you, comparing yourself to people who are running in a different race to you, and attempting to live up to ideas of who you think you are meant to be. You have spent so much time trying to edit yourself to fit in that you haven't taken the time to look beneath the surface and discover the magnificence that already exists within you.

In doing this, you are missing out on the blessing of YOU. You are missing out on all that you are capable of doing, being, and becoming. You are missing out on your unique path of purpose and accomplishment. You are missing out on the chance to know yourself, love yourself, and be yourself. And, coincidentally, you are also missing out on what it feels like to be loved as your authentic self. As Carl Jung stated, "The privilege of a lifetime is to become who you truly are."

I'm sure that, at some point in the past, you have made a snap judgement about a person after spending only a few minutes with them. But, after getting to know them, you realised that they were not who you thought they were based on external appearances alone. Perhaps you thought they looked like a dropout and then found out that they were a gifted musician. Or perhaps you thought they looked unintelligent only to discover that they are a genius. Maybe you thought they seemed conservative and boring only to realise that, actually, they are one of the most interesting people you have ever met.

We know that it is not wise to judge a book by its cover, so why do we do it with ourselves? Why are we so quick to assume that we aren't as beautiful, smart, or powerful as the people we look up to? Why do we rule ourselves out instead of taking the time to explore our hidden talents, gifts, and abilities? This is precisely what undermines our dreams: ignorantly writing ourselves off as ordinary instead of persisting until we discover just how infinitely inspiring and precious we are.

It is time to begin basing our sense of value and worth on something far deeper. We need to start looking within ourselves for the power, beauty, and magnificence we seek, instead of comparing ourselves to photoshopped images in glossy magazines. And, it is time to realise that our opinion of ourselves matters far more than a judgement anyone can make about who we are or what we do. If we don't, we will spend our entire life waiting for the people around us, God, or the world around us to tell us that we matter as a human being - that we are everything we dream of and more.

Think about it now: where does your sense of self-worth come from? Are you basing it on the sum total of your achievements to date? On the relationship you have today or those you have had in the past?

On the praise you receive from your teachers, mentors, parents, or peers? On the social circles you mingle in and the people you associate with? On the number of followers on your online profiles? Or, are you looking beyond external appearances alone to discover how unique and remarkable you are?

What you see in yourself today is just the tip of the iceberg of who you are, and there is so much more to discover yet. If you stop berating yourself for a moment, you will connect with the talents and gifts within you; the very expression of which is your destiny. You will experience a deep reverence for what makes you who you are, instead of spending your life wishing you were more like someone else.

In doing so, you will find the self-love and determination you need to achieve your goals, no matter how audacious they may seem, and back yourself in times when you need it the most. You will do whatever it takes to make your dreams manifest.

The forces that created you didn't sit above the Earth and say, "This one won't be as extraordinary as the others," when it designed you. It didn't put you on the planet and then say, "Whoops, messed that one up." So often, we question whether we are good enough, perfect enough, or just 'enough'. We judge ourselves, blame ourselves, hold ourselves back, and give up on what truly matters to us. And yet, at your core, you are made of the same stuff as every other human being: pure, untapped potential.

Therefore, life knows that we are worthy - it's us that doesn't. It doesn't question whether we are innately valuable; it knows without a shadow of a doubt that we are. It doesn't decide that we are undeserving of success because we're too short, too tall, too old, or too young; it planned us that way. Instead, it keeps encouraging us through signs and guiding us through little whispers to step forwards boldly and be exactly who we were born to be.

But, it's on us to make the first move. It's on us to love ourselves fearlessly for all that we are instead of believing that we are inferior in some way. It's on us to focus on our strengths instead of obsessing over our weaknesses. And, it is 100% our responsibility to stop measuring our worth based on social opinion and start finding it within ourselves instead.

What could you do today if you decided to cherish who you are? What could you achieve in your life, career, and your income if you expressed yourself the way your soul intended you to? What impact, influence, or change could you create in the world around you? And, perhaps more importantly, who could you inspire by being one of the rare human beings who appreciates and celebrates their originality?

Unrivalled personal power rests in your courage to be original and claim your unique role in the world. You are not just rare: you are one in seven billion. No one can be you, beat you, compete with you, or replace you once you own that. It's what enables you to find your competitive advantage and play your winning hand in life by doing what you do best and love the most. It is by willingly embracing all that is ugly and beautiful and dark and light about you that you will begin to develop an essential sense of worth for who you are; a sense of worth based on your true authentic self, not on who you think you are supposed to be.

So, instead of trying to change who you are, find out who you are and realise that you are perfect to the core. You are not broken. You don't need fixing. You are not a waste of space. The world needs you. You were designed this way. These quirks, this personality, these qualities, and the calling that you can't silence within you, they are precisely what make you so magnificent. You are a work of art and it is time to realise that you truly are perfection made manifest, so that the world can benefit from the highest expression of your soul and your entire life can flourish in the process.

Honour Your Calling in Life

It intrigues me how and why we can become concerned with what other people think of who we are, what we do, and how we choose to live our lives. An esteemed colleague of mine, Dr Olivier Becherel, once commented that he believes the fear of being disliked or rejected stems from ancient herd psychology where, if you were rejected from your tribe, you would be left out in the wilderness and have to fend for yourself. When human life was more primal, belonging mattered greatly, as it was often a case of life or death.

However, in today's world, if you are rejected by your tribe - be it your family, your partner, your colleagues, or your social circle - it is rarely a threat to your physical existence. Even if it stings to be made an outcast or to no longer belong where you once did, you are highly unlikely to die from it.

In fact, in a great act of irony, being courageous enough to go against the grain is now vital if you are to be true to yourself and live an original life that is flooded with meaning and accomplishment. So, if we know that this is true, why do we sometimes place so much weight on the often unsolicited advice of people on how we ought to live, love, and work?

Becoming overly fixated on what our friends, family, and followers think of our actions and choices often has a detrimental impact on our personal fulfilment. If we are not conscious of who we are listening to when defining our future nor courageous enough to listen to what lies inside our hearts, we may end up living a life that feels empty. We may find ourselves building careers we don't care for, engaging in relationships that drain us, and aspiring for goals that bring us no meaning.

Furthermore, running around trying to please other people with your choices and actions is not only exhausting, it is also a game that you can't win. The further out of your way you go in an attempt to keep everybody around you smiling, the greater the sacrifices you will make. What you give up as you prioritise what others want over what your heart yearns to do will stack up, until you eventually begin feeling lost and directionless because you have now reached the point where you have lost touch with what inspires you. It's simply not worth it.

The life that you want for yourself exists on the other side of your willingness to value your own voice above what people say, as we can't know what our purpose is if we are too dialled into the opinions of others to hear ourselves think. This is why it matters greatly that you learn to listen to yourself and trust the nudges from within you, for they are guiding you to what is possible for you in life.

Is it true that sometimes we don't make the wisest decisions, and someone else's advice might have been more useful than our own? Yes, but I also believe that experiencing the trial and error of being human, and learning everything we can along the way, is how we master our lives. No one else can take our journey for us, and so it is sometimes only in embracing each experience fully that we can figure out who we are and create an authentic life for ourselves.

I had my fair share of questionable partners in my teenage years and early twenties. I dated one man in particular who my parents begged me to leave as he had cheated on me with several of my friends (my father nearly hit him with a didgeridoo when he showed up on our doorstep at 4:30 a.m. one morning). But, in reflecting on the deeper purpose of the relationship, I saw that the emotional distress I experienced gave me two significant gifts as a young woman.

The first was the profound epiphany that I deserved more. The second was the freedom to move on with my life, as I left home and relocated to a different city after I finally saw through him and ended the relationship. If I had listened to my parents' advice and dumped him months earlier, I might never have received those invaluable lessons that are still with me today.

Although seeking people's input on big life decisions can sometimes provide a sense of comfort, their opinions can't guide you the way the voice from within you can. In fact, what other people say can lead you away from your own path of purpose. This is why learning to trust yourself is vital because no one is more qualified than you are to know what feels right for your future, career, relationships, and financial status.

Do you trust that you can pick yourself back up if and when you fall? Do you trust that there is a greater plan for your life and that every twist and turn of your journey is helping you to fulfil that plan? Do you trust your intuition when it tells you where to go, who to spend time with, and how to spend your day? If you do, then you can create the life that inspires you the most. But, if you blindly follow the advice of other people and ignore what is within you, you could end up anywhere.

Ask yourself, where will their advice lead you? What kind of life are the people providing the advice living? Would you trade places with them if you were given the chance? Even if they have achieved goals you aspire to, listen to what they say with your intuition by your side. That way, you can decide if the guidance they provide will help you move closer to where you most want to be.

If you are willing to honour your calling despite outside opinion, it will set you free from a life spent trying to live up to someone else's expectations - expectations that hinder you from experiencing your own purpose. It will set you free from pursuing a career that your parents, teachers, or peers think you should follow - a career that you don't love with all your heart. Finally, it will set you free from unnecessary drama and relationships that don't inspire you. You will be free to be the one-of-a-kind individual you were born to be.

After all, how can you thrive if you are too busy bending your own principles to fight for what truly matters to you? You can't. And if you spend all your time, energy, and money trying to fit in, you might never receive your own approval, which is critical for your fulfilment. When was the last time you asked yourself how you feel about your life? About where your career is going? About the people you share your space with? Or what the next move for your business is? Your input matters greatly, so honour it. I dare you to break away from popular opinion and chart your own path forwards in life.

If I had listened to outside opinions when I felt compelled to put my university degree on hold, I would be a doctor or a lawyer today. I may have never found my true calling as a writer, and you wouldn't be reading this book right now. I wouldn't have experienced the power of personal development, founded a business, or discovered just how big an impact one human being can make on the planet when they are inspired from within. Thinking about the many people who wouldn't have received the inspiration they needed if I had ignored my calling certainly puts what other people thought about my choices along the way into a harsh and useful perspective.

I was young - just a teenager - when I decided to go out on my own. I had no qualifications or proof that I would be able to do what I wanted to with my life, but I was consumed by a dream and a vision of what I could do and who I could be. I knew that I was born to write, and I was determined to use my writing to make a difference for people.

All that I hold near and dear today was made possible because I didn't listen to career counsellors as a young adult and chose to honour the calling from within me, instead. I can only imagine what it must have been like to watch a young woman drop her university degree without a plan or a job. It seemed illogical looking in from the outside, but it made sense to me, and it has been by far the most rewarding decision I made.

While you might ask people for input on your direction and plans (friends, family, mentors, teachers, and coaches included), remember to come home to the voice that counts most: your own. If you make life decisions you think will impress other people, you will only let yourself down in the end, and no amount of approval from the outside world will make up for the deep regret you will feel when you wake up ten years from now and realise that you haven't started living for yourself yet. This is why it is vital that you make sure you have the first and final say in all pursuits that matter.

Remember: rejecting yourself and your calling will hurt far more in the long run than having your choices rejected by someone else today. The cost is far greater than you can imagine. Their opinion is just one moment in time, but this is your whole life. So, be bold. Choose how you want your future to be, and then go to great lengths to make it all that it can become.

Go Your Own Way

As a child, I was convinced I had weird parents. In fact, on a handful of occasions, I felt embarrassed to be part of my family. While I experienced many blessings growing up, including homes in beautiful places and travel, I belonged to a family that did not fit into the mould in any way, shape, or form. We drove a Peugeot 504, rarely ate junk food, and sat in front of a television screen less than half an hour a day.

My mother was interested in cultivating original thinking in me. So, she provided toys that stimulated my imagination. My childhood was full of Lego, pencils, paper, books, crafts, train sets, dress-up clothes, cooking, and nature, which fed my creativity and taught me to be innovative from a young age (I dressed up as a blueberry once). My father has been known as an eccentric character who hasn't ever been particularly interested in what other people think about him, the way he lives, or how he dresses, for that matter.

For the most part, we didn't follow the trends of the families and kids at the schools I attended. As a result, I often felt incredibly uncool during my school years (it won't surprise you to know that I hated this as a teenager). But, as it turned out, it taught me a valuable lesson that shaped the woman I am today: a lesson about the power of going your own way.

To this day, I am thankful that my parents had the courage to be authentic instead of putting on an image just to fit in. By doing this, they showed me that being willing to honour who we truly are is a great and undervalued secret to a life that is full to the brim with depth, purpose, and meaning.

You can go along with the crowd and feel like you belong, but what happens when what the crowd is doing doesn't inspire you? What if settling down with a house and kids isn't for you? Or what if the lifestyle other people enjoy doesn't interest you? Taking this a step further, what if you suddenly realise that you flat-out disagree with the way that your peers live their lives? What then?

Sometimes going with the grain makes sense, like when you are researching for the best product to buy or deciding where to go on holiday. But when it comes to decisions that will impact your entire future, following the crowd is a fast-track towards feeling lost, confused, and unfulfilled.

Do you think that Albert Einstein lived a socially acceptable or predictable life? Or what about Picasso, Galileo, Marie Curie, Rockefeller, Martin Luther King Jr, Gandhi, or Joan of Arc? Many of the people who shaped the world we live in today were challenged and rejected while pursuing their vision. Some were even killed or burned at the stake for their relentless devotion to their path. But, look at what they accomplished because of their courage to stand up for what they believed in. They chose to go their own way, no matter the cost.

In 2002, Elon Musk received $180 million for the sale of Paypal. He invested the funds into SpaceX and the start-up of Tesla, determined to make human life on Earth more sustainable. What many people don't know is that, during this time, he had to borrow money for rent. Most people would stop working altogether if $180 million landed in their lap, but Musk had bigger plans. He was determined to prolong the future of the human race by improving environmental sustainability and providing us with an exit strategy for a planet that may soon become uninhabitable. What seemed crazy to many seemed sane to him.

The way I see it, people who go their own way are far more interesting, creative, and likely to make an impact than those who remain trapped by popular opinion. Wouldn't you prefer to have a circle of friends who boldly follow their soul than people who are too timid to claim who they are and what they care about? Friends like this will leave you with far fewer excuses for holding back on what you feel called to do.

One look at the world around you will show you that the majority of people feel unfulfilled and empty and that only a few are thriving. Which side do you want to be on? If you follow what the majority of people do, you will end up living the way the majority of people do. You will say yes to things you don't want to do, work a job you dislike, and end up in places you never wanted to be. In short, you'll be living someone else's life.

I don't believe for one second that this is what you want for yourself, and if summoning the courage to go against the grain is what it takes to fulfil your destiny, then choose to be 100% in: signed up, opted in, determined, and committed. The 'outside-the-box' life is the one for you and I, because it's the richest one of all.

So, become more concerned with whether you are following your purpose than whether your life matches up to societal expectations. Care more about whether your direction is based on what is true, real, and honest for you than whether you fit in while pursuing it. Place more weight on how fulfilled you are personally than wondering whether your workplace, school, church, or family approve of the way you live. That is the only way you can serve humanity well by being who you are.

I once mentored a client who had chosen to follow the entrepreneurial path and start a business. During a session, he mentioned to me that he had noticed how different he was from his family. He had recently attended a gathering where he had become acutely aware of the stark contrast between his views on life and how his relatives viewed the world. His goals and aspirations for the future were far removed from what many of his family members aspired for, and he seemed a little unsettled by it. In his words, he had realised that he was an anomaly.

"You're right - you *are* an anomaly," I told him. I encouraged him to embrace it, for it is in discovering what is unique about us that we simultaneously discover what is magnificent about us as well as the destiny we were born for. I then explained how the upheaval and transformation of personal relationships often happens when a person discovers the purpose of their life and chooses to pursue it instead of settling for the status quo. People you've known for years drift away and new people who are more aligned with where you are going show up to take their place.

I suggested that he find his 'family of freaks': a community of people who understood and appreciated him and who he could express all of himself with. Just one month later, during our next session, he told me about the inspiring people he had met on a recent international trip. It was clear that he had found his family of freaks and was on his way to living authentically.

I'm sure that you can relate to the feeling of being different - because you *are* different. And I am sure you have encountered moments when you felt out of place, convinced that you didn't belong. Maybe you feel that way in this very moment. Maybe you are completing a degree but being at university feels unnatural to you. Maybe you are working in a job where you are keeping your dream locked up inside you. Or maybe you are spending time with people who have smaller aspirations than you. That unsettled feeling, which tells you that you don't fit in, is your soul speaking to you. It is prompting, encouraging, and guiding you to break away; to follow what is inside your heart and find the life that fulfils you.

When you take a stand for that life, you will find your tribe; your family of freaks. You will attract people who love you for all that you are, in your purest, truest form, and find yourself engaging in more meaningful relationships in every area. And those relationships? They are worth their weight in gold.

In fact, I am certain that even one relationship where you share in heart-opening and mind-expanding conversations is worth far more than ten relationships where you force small talk just to avoid being alone. Those people will embrace all sides of you, stand by you in your darkest hours, support you to achieve your goals, and celebrate with you when you win. Therefore, any discomfort you feel by being an outsider in the short term will be worth it when you find them.

As I shared earlier, I struggled to fit in at school, especially during my secondary years. I was socially awkward, considered a bit of a geek and, up until around age 16, didn't have a great fashion sense (I committed many fashion faux pas I'm thankful I don't have photos of). Because of this, I often had closer relationships with my teachers than the students in my grade which, as you can imagine, only compounded the common perception that I didn't belong in the same social circles as the popular kids.

The few friends I did have were also outsiders who were anything but mainstream. I was accepted by a few and judged by many. While this felt like emotional torture during the sensitive years of puberty, it turned out to be a great blessing. It was truly magnificent work on life's part, as it was during this exact time that I discovered my love of writing and, simultaneously, my authentic self.

By being willing to tolerate the agony of social rejection, I developed a formidable relationship that many people do not get to experience: a relationship with my purpose. That's what happens when you decide to be true to yourself instead of trying to fit in with the crowd. You discover all that is within you and what you were born to do. You discover why you are here and your destiny on Earth.

It's impossible to create a life that is full of meaning by trying to live up to shallow images that look good to the outside eye. And therefore, the pain of breaking the status quo to travel in your own lane pales in comparison to the burden of the heavy regret you will carry if you keep putting off the life that you want to live. So, my question to you is this: are you willing to opt out of the races that don't matter in pursuit of your true path? Are you willing to sacrifice what is popular for the calling that lights you up from within?

Yes, it takes courage to go against the grain, but the rewards of following your own flow are worth every growing pain you will experience along the way. Why? Because nothing is more satisfying than waking up in the morning to a life that you love; the one you hand-crafted to fulfil your dreams, one that is overflowing with unlimited inspiration, extraordinary experiences, and soulful moments. So, continue to live in alignment with your highest inspiration, truth, and wisdom, no matter how much inner strength it might sometimes take.

No one can follow your path of purpose and claim your destiny for you, and so it's on you to choose it, surrender to it, and allow your heart to guide you to fulfil it. Go your own way, even if that means walking alone, and follow your heart and soul to great places. If the music moves you, dance. If the trip calls to you, go. If the business idea is within you, launch it. Live your life unedited by the voices of the outside world and don't change who you are for anybody but you.

*****

It is human instinct to blend in or fly under the radar to survive, but you were not put on the planet to just survive. You were put here to thrive. And, if you are going to do that - thrive in every way possible - then you must dig deep and harness the courage to be yourself. If you follow common advice, you'll live a common life, and you were born for so much more than this.

So, give yourself the permission and freedom to be different; to be the one-of-a-kind that you are. Don't hold your greatness back because other people can't handle it, don't understand or can't relate to it, or are even scared of it because they are fearful of shining their own light. Accept that not only can you be great but that you were born great. Let go of the fear of what others might say and be yourself without hesitation.

3

Unleash Your Greatness

"Never underestimate the power of dreams and the influence of the human spirit. We are all the same in this notion: the potential for greatness lives within each of us."

Wilma Rudolph

How do we reach a point where we are clear on who we are, where we are going, and why we were born? Where we feel that the actions we take and the decisions we make are aligned with the higher plan for our life? Where we are sharing our talents and touching lives all over the world?

Firstly, understand that no one can stop you from achieving your dream unless you allow them to. Regardless of what a parent, friend, partner, relative, or teacher has said in the past, you have the capacity for brilliance within you. Secondly, understand that nothing you have done or can do will ever make you unworthy of a life spent in pursuit of your purpose.

And lastly, understand that you can choose to find and express your greatness, every single day. It is the choice to believe that you are extraordinary, even when you are questioning if you have what it takes to fulfil your destiny. It is the choice to believe with endless faith that it is possible to live a life you love, even if you stumble or fall short along the way. And it is the choice to focus on building the future that inspires you, no matter what happened yesterday. It's time to set free the greatness within you and watch as your life takes on a whole new level of magic and meaning.

Fill Your Cup Until it Overflows

You are capable of doing incredible things in this world. But here's the thing: you can't make a mark on the planet, go on national television, write a best-selling book, launch a global movement, or speak up for your message if you are breaking apart on the inside.

Why? Because every single one of your achievements, be it personal or professional, is an expression of you. Therefore, when you start to flourish, your life will start to flourish. This journey begins with a commitment to make your spiritual, mental, and physical well-being a priority, every single day. The foundation of this well-being is a connection to and relationship with your purpose.

Without the central theme of your purpose running through each moment of your life, you will start to feel empty on the inside. The days will begin to feel like a blur, foods that you once enjoyed will lose their full flavour, and the world might start to look less beautiful than before. Your life will gradually be taken over by seemingly random and uninspiring chaos, from cars breaking down to ongoing money struggles to a long line of romantic relationships that don't work out.

You will have no idea where you are going, much less why you are going there. Because of this, your career and finances will flatline or enter a steep decline. A feeling of apathy about the future will grow.

Groundhog Day will turn into Groundhog week, month, year, or even decade. You might find yourself feeling alone and disconnected as you begin to grapple with your own existence and wonder what the point of it all is. From this place, the chances of fulfilling your potential and experiencing the greatness within you are slim to none. After all, how can you leave your footprints in the sand if you barely want to get out of bed in the morning?

Living in alignment with your purpose will create a radically different experience of being alive. Our purpose is the reason we are here at all, and because of this, it is also the source of our life force and physical well-being. If we feel that the future has nothing to offer us, we start to feel tired. Our body begins to break down, like someone switching off the light inside a room.

The longer we live without the vitality that pursuing our purpose brings, the more unwell our bodies become. This often happens for people who leave their career behind and enter retirement; the absence of purpose brings death closer. Simply put, if we aren't connected with our reason to live, we begin to die inside, but if we feel that our life is full of deep meaning, then great healing and miracles become possible.

Imagine if you were in the same place in five years' time, earning the same income, working the same job, or perhaps living in the same home you are now. This would more than likely bring about a feeling of dread because you know to your core that you were born for more. That insatiable pull from within you keeps urging you to grow; to build on today for tomorrow, to make progress, to develop, to become stronger, faster, and wiser. You want to know that what you do today has relevance in the big picture of your life and that you are moving closer to what you want to achieve and experience.

In your heart, you know that you weren't put here to settle for an empty existence. Like all human beings, you want to live a life where you approximate the highest level of Maslow's Hierarchy of Needs, which is self-actualisation. Self-actualisation is the place where you become all you can be, do all you can do, and achieve all you are capable of in every area. The closer you move towards this place, the more alive your mind, body, and spirit will become, and the more inspiring each day will be.

I have long believed that feeling depressed is the result of one or more of the following. The first is a lack of clarity about where we are going in life. That is, not having a sense of direction for the future. The second is a perception that we are insignificant or invisible, and that who we are and how we live doesn't matter to the world. It is feeling that we are not worthy of the connection and accomplishment we desire. The third is when we experience a problem that we can't see a solution for; questions we don't have answers to or a mystery we can't seem to solve.

Living in line with our purpose heals all three of these underlying causes of feeling down and out. When you find your purpose, you know what you would love to spend your life and doing and thus, the direction you want to move in. You realise that both who you are and what you do matters. And finally, the vision you see for the future gives you a reason to overcome every obstacle you face on the path to creating it.

Purpose quells the feeling that life isn't worth living, because when you become ignited from within, you not only discover how much magic there is to be seen and felt in the world, but you also discover all that you were born to be. And, by focusing on where you want to go and what you want to achieve in your lifetime, you will fulfil your potential, one day at a time.

Maybe you don't feel ready to pursue your purpose or blaze a trail in the world yet. Perhaps you feel too sensitive to handle the opinions of the people you might meet along the way. Maybe you are still too busy trying to understand your past to create a new future. Maybe the thought of all of the above just feels like too much at this point. And so, you don't feel that you've got it in you to share your gifts and express your greatness yet.

If this is true for you, then know that it is okay, and you are okay. I spent the better part of a year doing personal development daily in a quest to know, understand, and love myself before I felt ready to serve the world. I wanted to work on my own life first before I helped others do the same.

Reading mountains of self-help books and attending courses - from Neuro-Linguistic Programming to chanting in the rice fields of Bali - cultivated my self-awareness and spirituality. It gave me the chance to find peace in my past and inspiration for my future so that I could move forwards with courage and confidence.

What happens during the transformation that deep healing work brings is life-changing. The noise around you will be silenced. You will connect deeply with your true self, and the love that you feel as you do will fill you up from within in ways you have never experienced before. And, as you continue to peel away the layers of your unresolved emotions, all that will remain is the purest expression of your soul on Earth; what you were born to do.

The healing you experience will bring with it a clear mind and new ideas. Your enthusiasm for life will be renewed and your spirit will be rekindled. If you do enough of it, you will reach a tipping point where your future is no longer defined solely by the events of your past, like history repeating itself to complete itself. It will be directed by your soul and the calling that lives inside you instead. The desire to run away from pain will dissolve and your life will become a great adventure of exploring and expressing all that you are and can be.

Even if you already have a long line of accomplishments behind you today, you still need the relief, release, and renewal that deep and transformative personal growth provides. To reach the next level, you need to be ready for the next level, and not just in terms of your knowledge and skills, but personally. And so, prioritising your personal healing is essential if you want to turn your life into one that you can't wait to live.

With every wound you heal from the past, the power of your actions will be amplified. With every fear you break through, your voice will be heard by more people. With every insight you gain about yourself, your work will increase in impact. You will become living proof of what happens when you let go of all that you are not and leave only the essence of who you are behind. Your investment in your personal healing will empower you to reach new heights, cross greater terrains, and make your unique difference in people's lives.

Inspiration for accomplishment, for living, and for a greater future is all around us, except most people are too glued to their technology or caught up in their lives to notice it. It's in the sky, as the sun rises and sets to mark the start and end of each day. It's in the stars and the moon at night. It's in the flowers as they burst into colour in the spring and in the leaves of the trees as they fall before winter. It's in the city lights, the ever-flowing rivers, and the majestic mountains of the world.

It's in the view of the Earth below when you are flying at 30,000 feet. It's in the great feats achieved by humanity; the scientific breakthroughs being made, the businesses serving millions of people, the timeless art being created, and the new athletic records being set. There is no shortage of it once you open yourself up to it. So, let it in. Let life in.

Draw on every source of inspiration you can find and use it to make your spark burn brighter, and when the inspiration that you feel is so deep and overwhelming that you cannot wait to express what is within you, get out there and make your contribution to the planet, too. Let your cup overflow and touch the lives of those around you. Let's make the world our stage and set people's hearts on fire.

Overcome Your Obstacles

It is inevitable that you will face adversity in your life. That adversity might show up in the form of a relationship ending, a health problem, a career hurdle, an unanswered existential question, or a complete personal breakdown. You might feel that nothing is going your way, that the cards are rarely played in your favour, or that life has gotten the better of you.

Perhaps you've had one of those weeks, months, years, or decades where you have been tested in every possible way, and it feels like you've been in the ring with Mike Tyson. Maybe it has left you raw and wondering how you are going to keep your chin up and make it through. You might even be contemplating whether life is worth living.

I get it. Sometimes life can feel like a game you can't win, and there is no doubt that being human isn't always easy. But here's the thing: it is in the moments where you feel like you cannot go on anymore that you must decide whether you will let your challenges derail you or fuel you, because how you face, embrace, and find grace in your obstacles is what determines how your story ends.

Many people are walking around with their spirit weighed down by the challenges they have encountered. You can see it in the lines on their face, sense it in the way they slump their shoulders, and hear it in the way they speak. It's like the wind has been knocked right out of their sails. This doesn't have to be you. You can use the adversities you face as a stepping stone on your way to the top.

I've heard many stories from people who have overcome tragedy and heartbreak where they told me that not only did they manage to find a way through the darkness, but that in doing so, they connected with the guiding light of their purpose for the first time. They shared that the extreme adversity they once struggled with led them to a life greater than anything they dreamed could be possible. I am certain that the same can be true for you, and if you look for the cracks of light shining through the darkness, you will find it: a way out, a way through, and the start of a whole new future.

So, if you feel like you have reached rock bottom right now, rest easy. It is not a terrible place to be. In fact, it may be the opportunity that you've been waiting for; the opportunity to start over, set goals that inspire you, and shape your life the way you desire. The lowest points you face on your journey can bring with them profound clarity about who you are and what you want; two things many people never find, and thus are never able to live the way they desire.

The fire of adversity burns away everything that doesn't matter and leaves behind only that which does. It breaks down the old so that new life can sprout. It puts events and people into perspective. It helps you to discover your purpose and, if you let it, it can leave you standing stronger than ever before. It can awaken the ambition you need to shape up, show up, and kick ass. It can be the motivation you need to stop letting trivial circumstances get in the way of grand pursuits and finally prioritise what you are here for.

If you read the story of any individual who has achieved great things, you will find that not only did they encounter defeat along the way, but that it was often that very same defeat that drove them to reach the top. In fact, had they not faced an extreme challenge like being beaten up, abused, or rejected, they might not have found and fulfilled their greatness at all. Because of this, they offer courage and hope to all those who are struggling. They show us what is possible if we refuse to give up when the seas are stormy.

You cannot build an extraordinary life while living with the assumption that you are wounded by the events of your past, nor can you create the career and wealth you want if you think that the world is against you. But if you believe that you are resilient and that life is helping you rise up, you will go to great places. Of this, I have no doubt. So, embrace the truth that we all have lessons to learn and focus on doing exactly that - learning, growing, expanding, and evolving - because regardless of how obstacles appear, their purpose is the same: to help us to do and become all that we are capable of.

Sometimes we think that we can become strong enough to protect ourselves from the pain that we never want to feel again. But, in truth, attempting to avoid pain is precisely what weakens us, because carrying yesterday's events into tomorrow is a heavy load to bear. What's more is that the heavier the load, the quicker it will wear you down.

If you go through life feeling bitter about all the little things that don't go your way, you will crumble when faced with a challenge worth conquering, as nothing weakens us or dulls our shine more than holding onto sadness, regret, fear, and self-righteousness.

The world will not always go easy on you when you want it to, it won't always be on your side when you want it to agree with you, and things won't always go your way. It will be what it is. The same principle applies in reverse: the world will not always be tough when you think it is going to be, nor will you always be rejected when you expect to be. Your job is to look for the beauty and opportunity that lies within each moment and develop resilience so that you know that not only can you emerge on the other side but that you can do so with renewed vigour, heart, and spirit.

Life is far more beautiful when you see it for what it really is. If you expect to face problems and grow as you move towards your goals, you will thrive. But if you are hell-bent against being left out, cheated on, or beat on, then that is often what you will get more of until you decide to face your fights with gumption.

Sometimes we forget that there is a greater plan for our life and that every event we experience is part of that plan. But, if you look closely, you will see the truth. You will understand why certain events happened the way they did and what your struggles were leading you towards. You will know why your ex-partner left you, why that company fired you, or why you failed that exam. Essentially, you will understand why your past had to unfold the way it did and why it couldn't have unfolded any other way, because then you wouldn't be who or where you are now.

You will feel grateful for the experiences that challenged you, because had your history been different, your path of destiny would be too. As you appreciate the deep divinity of your journey, your life will quickly become one where your toughest days are still far more meaningful than your life would ever have been had you let your dream become buried under the pain of the past.

Bullying and near-suicidal depression were just the beginning of the struggles I have encountered while chasing my dream. I experienced several relationship break-ups, leaving a partner behind in Canada knowing I was never going back, money struggles, sexual abuse, business breakdowns, and being ostracised by people I once considered friends. And so, I know what it is like to cry your heart out, to break open from the inside, and to feel alone, powerless, ashamed, misunderstood, insignificant, and vulnerable.

But to this very day, I am thankful for these obstacles as each one has pushed me to go further, dig deeper, and reminded me to never, ever believe that it is over, even when I am close to giving up. They are part of my journey and the very reason I do what I do. I wouldn't be who I am without them, and it is because I have stood in the fire and been burned that I found myself, my mission, and my voice at all.

We are hindered by the challenges we are yet to find the blessing in and fuelled by those we have. It is a huge cost to pay, to keep holding onto the idea that we are a victim of what we experience, as we cannot shine our light if we are hiding in the shadows of our past, nor help others find the hope they need if we haven't found it for ourselves yet. Similarly, we cannot become who we are born to be and live the life that we are capable of until we have put our personal adversities into a greater perspective.

And so, learning to heal and become strong in the face of adversity is essential if you are going to move forwards with confidence and vigour. I've seen what happens for people when they realise that what they thought challenged them actually set them on the path that life intended for them all along. It's extraordinary, radical, awe-inspiring, and breathtaking, and it can happen for you.

Life is a ride. As you grow, you will face trials and tribulations and tough decisions. Your purpose will keep calling you forward to greater places and bigger achievements, and you won't be able to carry all your baggage with you as you go. So, don't bench yourself because you stumbled once, twice, or even ten times. That's called a learning curve. Don't rule yourself out because you aren't where you want to be yet. That's called the path of mastery. Don't decide that you weren't born great because you were kicked out of home, had a drug addiction, or failed an exam in school. That's called the magnificent story of your life unfolding.

The power of the human spirit to transcend challenge is extraordinary, and what happens when we connect with that spirit is astonishing. We are far greater than we realise, and it is often in our most challenging times that we discover what we are made of. It is when we are faced with difficult situations that we learn who we are and what matters the most to us, and it is when we break open from the inside that the greatness within us emerges.

So, whatever is challenging you today, face it, heal it, and know to your core that you can turn any losing hand into a winning one once you realise that life truly is working on your side. For every problem, there is a solution. For every challenge, there is an opportunity. For every question, there is an answer. For every crisis, there is a blessing. The trial comes before the triumph and struggle often precedes success.

Remember that you are never given a challenge without the ability to move through it, and you are never thrown in the deep end without a rope. So, make today the day that you find a way to turn your adversity into an advantage and start the next phase of your journey feeling loved, whole, strong, and complete.

Don't let the road get you down. Keep your head and heart focused on where you want to go, and soon the bumps you face will become just another plot twist in the great story of your life. They will be potholes that made you stronger, rough surfaces that prepared you to scale the mountain, and puddles that reminded you to revel in the miracles that happen along the way.

Let nothing you face from this moment forwards stop you from believing that you can live a phenomenal life. Instead, be the person who can find a silver lining in even the darkest of clouds, because no challenge you encounter is worth giving up on the great adventure of your destiny.

Say 'I Do' to Your Purpose

It is a natural part of our human search for fulfilment to seek an intimate relationship. We want a partner to sleep beside at night, to grow with, face challenges with, and share our life with. Deep down, we long to be seen, heard, felt, and loved for who we are. Along with this desire is a yearning to share the same unconditional love with the one we care about. We want to love them in their light and in their darkness, encourage them to achieve their dreams, and be a listening ear when they need it.

This desire to love and be loved is intense and, as stories of romance show us, people will go to great lengths for the mate they seek (for example, the history of the Taj Mahal). There is no doubt that there is great meaning and magic to be found and felt in the world of intimate relationships; connection, communication, and companionship included. The challenge arises when, in this search for a special someone to share our heart, time, and space with, we neglect two relationships that are crucial for an extraordinary life: the relationship with ourselves and the relationship with our purpose.

I spent many years trying to change who I was for the sake of a relationship. I flew across the world for a man I'd never kissed, moved cities several times to be with a partner, and was skilled at attracting unavailable men. I pursued many potential mates that anyone could have told me in a heartbeat were never going to be a match for me. Nonetheless, I kept persisting as I was yearning for a significant other to love and appreciate me as a woman.

I had ended yet another relationship when I finally felt the impact of the sacrifices I had been making by trying to make myself and my life fit with the partners I had chosen. When it didn't work out - which, when I was honest with myself, I knew it wouldn't, right from the start - it often took weeks or months to clean up the mess the relationship had created. Each time, I had to work hard to find my way back to myself and move on with my life, all because I had compromised what mattered to me for the sake of sex, company, and compliments.

It was only when I realised that no man, regardless of how wealthy, successful, or attractive he might appear to be at first glance, was worth giving up on my dream for. That was the moment when my love for myself became greater than the love I'd felt for any partner. I began prioritising my long-term fulfilment over temporary lust and choosing relationships that served my highest mission and purpose. My career took off in the years that followed this epiphany, and I haven't put my ambitions on hold for intimacy since.

No intimate connection can fulfil you the way your relationship with yourself and your purpose can. Despite this, so many people look for their 'other half' in a spouse, hoping to meet 'The One' and never again feel alone. They assume that true love can only be found and felt in the arms of a partner, and so they try to find the person they believe completes them; the person they feel makes life worth living.

This endless search for a 'happily ever after' can cause us to ignore the problems we are facing in our own lives, like not knowing what our next move is in our career or needing to get our ducks in a row for the future we want. While what we learn in our romantic relationships can undeniably help us to discover who we are and develop our confidence, they often provide us with a shallow sense of security and self-esteem that ends when the relationship does. Essentially, it is a band-aid solution in place of the empowerment and reward that deep personal reflection and growth brings.

Placing how fulfilled you are in the hands of your relationship will leave you vulnerable, as you can't control anyone's actions except your own. If you do, you will feel down when they are down, be emotional if they don't call when you want them to, and even find yourself trying to 'fix' or change them instead of appreciating them for who they are. Their life will become the centre of your life.

Their opinion might start to matter more than your own, causing you to ignore what your heart and soul wants to do. You could waste precious time worrying about whether they are heading down a similar road to you, which often isn't the case as we each have our own journey to take to fulfil our destiny. If you overstay your welcome in a relationship that doesn't inspire you, for fear of feeling alone or because you don't know who you are, you may become increasingly dependent and disempowered: the fast-track to a break-up.

The ripple effect of the relationship ending can be far-reaching. You might experience a loss of confidence, question your attractiveness and worth, face financial struggles or a change in your living situation, and experience a drop in your productivity in your career. It can even have an impact on your friends and family or cause you to lose your enthusiasm for life. How quickly and smoothly we move forwards after separating from a partner depends on how we navigate and manage all of the above, including how we lay our personal emotions about the relationship to rest.

In times where you find yourself single once more - just me, myself, and I again - the fastest path to healing is to return to what you love to do. It is to get back to what matters most to you, reconnect with your purpose, take bold steps towards your goals, and focus on creating the life you want for yourself. And for the sake of your future and your well-being, to strengthen your sense of self so that next time a partner comes along, you won't give up everything that matters to you to spend time with them.

We only tolerate incompatible partners and settle for unfulfilling relationships when we aren't sure of who we are or where we are going. Therefore, if you work on these every day, then bending on things you know are deal-breakers for you will soon become a habit of the past. No longer will you try to change the track of your own life to journey alongside someone else's (which will only have you end up returning to who you are anyway). Instead, you will focus on the beauty that is around and within you, and only accept relationships that fulfil and inspire you.

We are each on a unique path of evolution, and so by default, human relationships will always seem a little bit, or very, messy. The key to navigating through them is to remember that, regardless of who the person is, they are just a human being and, therefore, it is impossible for them to fulfil all your dreams and desires. But your relationship with your heart, your soul, your purpose, and your calling? That relationship is the most sustainable and stable one you will ever find.

It is there for you 24 hours a day, seven days a week, without fault or failure. It will fill your life with meaning, draw incredible opportunities towards you, and open doors to new and wonderful lands. It will heal you, guide you, drive you, and fulfil you. It is the deepest source of the appreciation you seek, and in my experience, it is also the pathway to the greatest love you can feel: the love of life, the love of being alive, and the love of who you are.

You don't need to sacrifice who you are to find a soulmate, and your other half isn't missing; you are already whole and complete. No one knows you the way that you do, and you are the person you spend your entire life with, from birth to death. So, work on that relationship, each and every day. Get to know yourself intimately, learn to love yourself unconditionally, and grow the career, the wealth, and the future that moves you.

You are not alone in the universe. You never have been, never are, and never will be. So, instead of seeking support from one special someone, realise that you are that special someone. Allow life to support you on your path. Trust that the road will rise up to meet you. Let humanity become your family. Find your soulmate in the sun, the stars, the earth, and the trees. Great gifts await you, and love is all around you.

By finding a sense of belonging within you - within your purpose and calling - your relationships will be more fulfilling than ever before. You will find yourself surrounded by people who love you dearly. You will share in meaningful conversations every day. From this place, the intimate relationship that you seek, the one that empowers you to conquer your goals and see the world, will manifest right before your eyes. As Dr John Demartini said, "The fastest way to find someone who matches you is to be you."

*****

Unleashing your greatness won't happen overnight. It is a journey that unfolds, one moment and one day at a time. Every time you take a step in the direction you want to go, you awaken it. Each time you make time for your purpose, you unfold it. Every time you overcome an obstacle that stands between where you are today and the vision in your mind, you ignite it.

So, become more committed to discovering the potential within you instead of buying into stories that you don't have the capacity for greatness. Become more invested in seeing your life take off than stacking the odds against yourself. Become an advocate for your goals, your dreams, your wildest ambitions, and your greatest aspirations. If you do, you will soon find yourself living the life that you deserve; the one that you are truly capable of.

4

Your Destiny Is Calling

"Twenty years from now you will be more disappointed by the things that you didn't do than the ones you did do. So, throw off the bowlines. Sail away from the safe harbour. Catch the trade winds in your sails. Explore. Dream. Discover."

Mark Twain

You might be asking yourself if a life that matters is possible for you. One where you be who you are, have what you want, and change the world. You might be wondering whether there really is a grand plan in mind for you, and not just one where you grow up, go to school, work a job, raise a family, then die. You are essentially asking if the 'rags to riches' story can happen for you, and whether you, too, can experience a transformation so significant that in just twelve months from now, your life is radically different from where you are today.

Do you know what the answer is? Of course, you do. You might question it at times, but when push comes to shove, you know the truth. You were born to do and experience extraordinary things, and as you discover what that looks like for you and commit to creating it, you will find your runway and take off to great places.

You don't have to hit the wall or encounter extreme adversity to begin living fully. You can do it right now. You can start today by asking yourself, "What touches my heart the most?" Then be willing to go all in on making sure your life - this life - is one that you cannot wait to live.

Discover the Deep Magic of Life

I was just a teenager when I connected with my dream to travel the world writing and speaking. Not only did I want to fulfil this dream, but I wanted to live and work in style along the way. By actively pursuing my purpose and doing what I loved to do, my life quickly became full of incredible experiences, very few of which I paid for out of my own pocket.

By the age of 25, I had toured the north island of New Zealand, stood on the Great Wall of China, visited Niagara Falls, lived in several countries, and eaten breakfast in Rodeo Drive. I had worked for clients who sent private cars to collect me, paid for dinners that would have broken my budget by a long shot, and arranged an all-expenses-paid working trip to a resort in Bali - meals, private villa, and four-poster bed included.

I had stayed in five-star hotels, seen breath-taking sights, ridden elephants, and eaten food that was like heaven in my mouth. Multimillion-dollar mentors had taken me under their wing and taught me the ropes in business. I had also been offered the opportunity to write and publish my first book, speak on stages, be interviewed on radio shows, and be the face of projects, documentaries, and brands I believed in.

If I had sat around wanting fancy hotels and private cars without also making my contribution to humanity, those experiences would have been nothing but hopes and wishes. But, because I was out there doing my thing in the world, I attracted an abundance of what my heart desired. People can feel it when you are inspired by what you do and when you care about something far greater than yourself; they want to be around you, get to know you, pay you, pay for you, be served by you, and bring opportunities your way.

My first book was launched in Auckland, New Zealand. Since the book attracted a significant investment from a corporate sponsor and featured an interview with the founder of the company, the official release coincided with their annual conference. This meant that the book was launched at an event with 250 people, many of whom had flown in from overseas to attend (half of the audience were Taiwanese and listening through translators, which meant that the laughter in response to my jokes occurred in two ripples: instantly, then 15 seconds later!).

But this part of my story isn't about the day that I achieved my dream of becoming an author. It's about something that happened during the launch that reminded me that when you follow the calling inside your heart, all of your dreams, both big and small, will come true.

I'm sure that you have watched television game shows where attractive women in shiny outfits hold briefcases full of cash for the winners. Well, a part of me wanted to do that too (who wouldn't want to hold thousands of dollars in their hands?). On the second night of the event, I was standing at the back of the room with my publisher, the business manager, and the company founder. They were about to issue cash bonuses to the highest performers for the previous year.

Then, guess what? The business manager handed me two suitcases, one containing $15,000 and the other $8,000, and asked me to go up onto the stage to hand the money to the recipients. Was this my grandest dream? Far from it. But was it an incredible experience? Absolutely. It taught me how magnetic we become when we follow our path and purpose with heart, no holds barred.

If you want to be valued by the world, offer value to the world. If you want to be treated like a VIP, then be a VIP to the world. But don't do it just because you want all the luxuries that come with it. Do it because you genuinely care about impacting people's lives. That is the key to the life that you're dreaming of. It isn't necessarily found in a mountain of self-help books. It's in getting out there and being someone greater for humanity.

Why? Because it is in doing so that you will discover all the magic that is within and around you. If you want to find your confidence, it's the answer. If you want to discover your true beauty, charisma, and magnetism, it's right there inside your calling. If you want to tap into your personal power, this is the way to unlock it.

Every single human being has their struggles, no matter how idealistic their life appears to be on the outside, and you can help those people by pursuing what is inside your heart. In fact, because you are reading this book, you are experiencing one of the greatest blessings of being alive today: the blessing of freedom.

You have the freedom to choose your profession and build a career you care about. The freedom to follow your calling, wherever and whenever it calls you. The freedom to study topics that interest you, to launch a business, grow an empire, start a movement. The freedom to speak your truth and stand up for what you believe in. The freedom to design, create, and live a life that inspires you. You are living with this freedom every single day, and every single day is a chance to use it for the benefit of yourself and the world.

Sometimes we forget that there are still millions of people alive today who do not have the freedom we do. Remembering this brings with it a humbling gratitude for the opportunity that we have to do what we love every day and craft our future, career, and life without restriction. It provides us with a necessary reality check on just how small our problems are in the grand scheme of things, and thus, how seemingly crazy it is to keep finding reasons why we can't succeed instead of seizing each and every moment as the opportunity that it is.

How limiting is it to believe that we cannot fulfil our dream because of something that happened last week, last month, or last year? Or because we don't like our hair, our body shape, our nose, our height, or our skin colour? What are we holding back by allowing these trivial excuses to distract us from what is right in front of us every single day? How crazy is it to do anything except make the most of all that we have been given?

We have no idea how much it matters that we pursue what is deep inside our heart nor how big a difference we can make by doing so. Simply put, you are surrounded by opportunities to thrive and you have everything you need right here and now to turn your life into a blessing for the world. You can write a book that gives hope to thousands. You can start a business that serves millions. You can teach others how to heal their bodies and regain their wellness. You can support families to build wealth for the future. You can travel the world, meeting thousands of people and encouraging them to live their dream.

I'm not saying that we are obligated to serve the world or that we must try to rescue the people in it. I'm simply inviting you to remember that you have freedom that is denied to many and that you can do something extraordinary with it. You can choose to make your life one of great meaning and significance, live by example, and show other people that they, too, can find and follow their purpose.

I am blessed. You are blessed. We are blessed. So, embrace that blessing for all that it is. Don't rob the world of what is inside you. Use today as an opportunity to fulfil your unique and inspiring role on the planet. Speak truths that empower and liberate others. Stand up for what you believe in, even if it is not popular opinion. Light up the world with your gifts.

Change an industry, people's lives, the way children are schooled, the monetary system, or the history books. Be free for all those who do not have the same privilege. Do it in honour of their souls and pave the way towards a brighter future. If you are willing to do this, then you will soon discover and experience the deep magic of life.

Your Life Is a Gift to the World

You are needed in the world. Your birth was not random. You were not a mistake. Even if you think you were, you weren't. You were planned. You were created on purpose and with a purpose in mind. If you feel any other way, it is only because you haven't connected with the significance of who you are yet.

As Mark Twain stated powerfully, one of the most important days in your life, besides the day you were born, is the day you work out why. That day will be an important turning point in your journey, as from that moment forward, you will no longer be able to question whether you and your life have significance in the grand scheme of it all.

Imagine for a moment all the people who are alive today: billions and billions of them, living in all the different countries across the planet. See their faces inside your mind. Imagine what they are doing today and who they are. Imagine their upbringing, their family structures, their beliefs and traditions. Imagine the problems they struggle with and the challenges they are facing. As you imagine, remember that inside each and every one of them is the desire for a greater life.

Now think about this: how is it possible that you don't have the power to make a difference to even a small handful of these billions of people? You can solve a problem that holds them back, help them find answers to important questions, and help them achieve a goal they care about. Why would life have it any other way? What would be the purpose of your existence if you didn't have something inside you that could be the very difference someone else has been waiting for?

We often underestimate the power and importance of our presence on the planet. As a result, we have no idea just how many lives we could touch if we chose to use what is within us for the benefit of humanity. But when you comprehend the sheer power of even a single action, it becomes difficult to keep believing that you are worthless or that you cannot change someone's life with what you do. A smile can change someone's day, a compliment can lift someone's spirit, and words of encouragement can give someone the confidence they need to keep going just as they are thinking about throwing in the towel.

Stop and take a closer look at the impact you are having on those around you. Put yourself in other people's shoes for a moment - and I don't just mean the shoes of one person, but the shoes of many people. The shoes of your spouse. The shoes of your friends and family. The shoes of the people you work with. The shoes of the people you walk past on the street or the cashier in the store. What influence are you having on them?

Every movement you make, every word you speak, and every action you take creates a ripple effect in the world around you. This is why it is impossible for you to not touch the lives of those who you cross paths with. Even if you only meet someone for a fleeting moment, your presence can affect them for years to come. I'm sure that you have experienced this, where someone appeared out of the blue and impacted your life forever; where their presence stayed with you or their words lingered in your mind long after you met them.

With this in mind, I invite you to meet yourself:

In all that you are,
In your capacity to lead, touch, move, and inspire,
In the difference you care enough to make,
And in the undeniable truth that you COUNT.

If you focus only on yourself, it will be easy to pick holes in who you are. It will be easy to focus on the credentials you don't believe you have, the money you think you are missing, and the features you find odd or unattractive about you. You will be able to list all the reasons why you think you are not cut out for the career you dream of and the ways you think you have failed or fallen short in the past.

Doing this will cause your confidence to drop through the floor and your belief in yourself to go out the window. As a result, you will give up before you make your big break, avoid situations where people might notice the things that you think make you insignificant, and settle for less than what you want. It is a life spent on the sidelines instead of getting on the field to play the game.

But, if you focus on what you have to offer to people and on using your gifts instead, everything changes. You will focus on what you have, not on what you don't. You will focus on where you can go, not on the reasons you think you can't go there. You will open up and connect with people instead of withdrawing and becoming closed off from the world. It is a life spent using your magic to create magic for others.

See, this isn't just about you. Your life doesn't exist just for you to live it. It exists so that the lives of others can be enhanced; so that people can evolve their own life through yours (and vice versa). It exists so that you can bring the talents that you have been blessed with to the forefront and share them. It exists so that you can rise up and empower other people to discover and fully express who they are too. By doing this, you will experience the true reward of being alive, which is to know what it feels like to serve another human being.

You discover your purpose by looking deep within yourself, but you fulfil your purpose by expressing it outwardly in the world, and once you realise how important it is that you do what you feel born to do, you won't hold back anymore. You will stop hitting the snooze button on your destiny. No longer will you question whether you can make a difference on the planet or underestimate how far your influence can reach. You won't waste a single day thinking that what you do and how you live your life doesn't count in the end, because you will know to your core that it does.

You are already far more important to people than you realise, and in more ways than you can imagine. But I also know that you are just scratching the surface of what is possible for you. So, why not expand your reach? Why not show the younger generations what is possible when we dare to get out there and give life a damn good shot? Why not encourage people to find their potential, too, so they don't die having never at least aspired for their dream, be it big or small?

If you give up on your dream, you send a message to the people around you that it is okay to settle for less than they deserve - and that includes those you love dearly. But if you make something truly remarkable of your time here, you can ignite the fire in the belly of thousands of people and give them permission to do the same. So, why not set your ripple effect in motion by living fully and doing all you can with all that you have been given?

There are people everywhere who need inspiration and courage to pursue their purpose; people who need to know what an incredible life looks like. So, make your presence count. Choose who you want to be and how you want to live. Act, talk, and walk with purpose and intention. Express what is deep inside your heart. As you do so, remember that you are anything but insignificant in this world. Otherwise, you would not have been born at all. Your impact matters. You matter.

You don't have to climb Mount Everest or start a billion-dollar company to know that your presence counts. The impact that you want to have on the planet starts right here. It starts in this moment. Making that impact is simply about finding your role to play, even if that is to create heart-opening music or incredible art or beautiful food. I'm not here to be a politician or a doctor or a scientist, but I can touch people with my words. That's what I care about most. What do you care about the most?

You can influence the lives of millions if you feel called to. You can touch the hearts, open the minds, and lift the spirits of people around the globe. You can share your musical abilities, your business acumen, your wealth of information, your voice, and your spiritual message with those who need it most. And, you can step forwards into the realisation that you are significant and that your presence on this planet is no mistake. Your life is a gift to the world. I'm sure of it.

Live Boldly in Pursuit of Your Dream

Have you ever caught yourself saying or thinking the following: "I want to fulfil my dream, but I need to do (x) first," "Following my heart is reckless," or "When (y) happens, then I'll be ready to do what I love." Very few people put their dream first. Most push it to the side, lock it up inside their heart, and let everything else get in the way of what they yearn to do.

They make what is happening today more important than the life they could be living tomorrow. They focus on responsibility instead of inspiration, logic instead of intuition, and limitation instead of vision.

Sooner rather than later, they find themselves feeling uninspired and depressed about their future. While I am all for making sure you have a roof over your head, I also know first-hand where leaping into the abyss can take you, accompanied only by a sense of something greater and a yearning for something more.

Why do we do this? Why do we let our dream fall to the bottom of the pile? Do we think that it is naïve to make life decisions with our purpose at the forefront of our mind? Do we believe that it's not possible to merge our work, heart, and income? Do we feel that what we would love to do isn't important to the world? Is that why we allow endless to-do lists to override what we feel called from within to do?

Perhaps we are afraid of what other people will think if we break away from the norm and start over from scratch. Or maybe it's because we don't think we have it in us to do something phenomenal, something incredible, something extraordinary. Or perhaps we fear putting ourselves out there, knowing that we could fail. It's a terrifying thought that can make us want to climb right back under the covers of our bed.

I don't need to tell you that the greatest rewards and experiences exist in living boldly in pursuit of what matters, because you already know that. You know that there is magic just waiting to happen in your life; magic that can only be seen and felt when you move courageously towards the future you desire. Not only this, you know deep inside you that you have what it takes to transform your life and make a meaningful impact on humanity. So, all that remains is to overcome whatever is stopping you from moving forwards and claiming that future for yourself, starting with the fear of the unknown.

It's true: you don't know how your life will pan out once you pull up anchor and leave the shore. You don't know whether your business will take off or nosedive into the ground. You don't know how the world will receive your talent, your artform, your ideas, your message.

You don't know what your loved ones will think as you take risks to make your dream come true. And you don't know how long it will take for you to earn an income doing what you love. You're right: there are no guarantees on what will or will not happen as you pursue your purpose.

But the predictability that you seek, which you think would make following your dream a safer pathway, doesn't exist. We are far more powerful than we realise, but we cannot predict the future. You don't know what events will make the news this month, what will happen in the lives of the people you care about this week, or what thoughts will enter your mind when you wake up tomorrow. That will be true regardless of whether you choose to consciously fulfil your purpose or not. And so, trying to know how everything will pan out in advance is impossible.

Furthermore, the pathway to fulfilling your destiny is not a linear process. Writing this book wasn't linear, stumbling upon my calling to write wasn't linear, and the breakthroughs that have impacted my career the most weren't linear. It would have been impossible for me to have told you where my journey would take me when I first started. All I knew was that I wanted to find out.

During a phone conversation many years ago, my father said to me, "Think about the greatest moments of your life." I paused and reflected on the critical turning points of my journey. Then he asked me, "How many of those did you plan?" I'm sure you can guess what my answer was: "None."

He reminded me that there is undeniably something greater at work in our lives, a force that is far beyond our imagination and comprehension. He reminded me that we will never know every step of the journey, regardless of how extensive our planning and preparation might be, and that it is only in moving forward fearlessly that the road rises up to meet us. That's when synchronicities happen; where you meet the right person at the right time, where opportunities are created, and where the signs and solutions you need cross your path at every turn.

So, trust in the truth that not only do you have what it takes to succeed, but that you were born for it. Life intended for you to shine in your own unique way. To know who you are and be it. To find your groove and rock it. To discover your destiny and fulfil it. The more you show up, willing and eager to learn and grow, the more magical the days of your life will become. This is what's really possible - so much more than we realise - and it is available for each and every one of us.

Perhaps you hold back from what your heart wants to do because you feel that it is selfish to put yourself first, chase your dream, and devote yourself to the goals that matter the most to you. And you know what? Maybe there will be people who think you are irresponsible or downright crazy for letting go of everything to take a risk for a vision only you can see. But here's a thought: what could you do for the people you care about once you fulfil that vision?

What could you do for your children when you are earning ten times the income you are now? What difference could you make in the lives of your friends if you stood on a global stage and shared your message? And what example could you set for future generations, both within and beyond your family lineage, by having the courage to try until you succeed?

You just never know who you will impact when you decide to live by example; what deep and lasting healing, radical self-love, great wealth, and amazing creations you might inspire in those around you when you follow your soul. As Gandhi was quoted to have said, "My life is my message."

In my defining moment at age 19 when I faced and overcame depression, I made a commitment to myself that I would do whatever it took to live an extraordinary life. I devoted myself to my dream with full surrender and relentless persistence, and I never gave up on the picture I saw in my mind of how my future could be.

I did this not because it sounded like a good idea or because someone told me to, but because there was no other option for me. Plan A was to thrive in pursuit of my purpose, and Plan B didn't exist. It was either life or death. That's how much it mattered that I made my dream my destiny.

What is the alternative for you? Imagine it now. What does the life where you ignore your heart look like? What does it feel like? And is it really an option? Holding back might feel like a safety net at times, but I can assure you, if you ever try to leap into it, it won't provide you with anywhere near the same sense of comfort as what you will experience if you go to sleep at night knowing that today, you made your life everything it could be and more… that today, you moved closer to the place you most want to be.

Nobody is dealt a picture-perfect hand in life, but it is the ones who dare to dream about a greater future who turn what many would accept to be a losing hand into a winning one. They allow their dream to call and guide them to far greener pastures, to the fulfilment of what their soul is destined to do on Earth. They let nothing stop them and stop at nothing on their path to the top. Take a moment now to imagine what could unfold if you, too, gave your goals your all. Truly amazing things can happen.

The best cure for the emptiness that we experience when we hesitate to pursue our dream is to DO IT; to courageously and boldly follow our calling to every place it takes us. You only have one life. This is it. It's happening within and around you. You're feeling it, breathing it, and living it. And in every single minute of the day, you are being guided to make the most of it.

You don't need anyone else's permission to be who you are and follow your dream. In fact, it's what the world is waiting for you to do. The permission that matters the most - the only permission that matters - is the one that comes from within you; the permission to live as fully and wholly as you can.

Yes, living in pursuit of your dream will require you to face your fears one by one, but who wants to live a life full of fear anyway? And yes, stepping into the spotlight will require you to love and appreciate yourself deeply, but who wants to go through life blaming and shaming themselves? And yes, finding out what your purpose is might take time, but who wants to live for 60 odd years and not at least try to find out what they are truly made of?

I am sure you will join me in saying that you have no intention of living an ordinary existence, which is what happens when we remain caught up in fear and self-doubt. If you haven't already started creating your extraordinary life, then today is the day to start focusing on the reasons you can be, do, and have all that you want instead of the reasons you cannot. Today is the day to believe wholeheartedly in your destiny and decide that you will chase your dream with all you have.

Choosing to courageously chase my dream even when it made no sense to the untrained eye or when I had no idea how it would work out - just that it would - has been the greatest blessing, beyond all doubt. Since then, I have discovered just how much of a gift life is, and it truly is a gift. It is a chance to feel alive in every way, a chance to express what is inside your heart, and a chance to change, touch, and inspire the world by being who you are. It is your opportunity to to find out what you love to do and do it, every single day.

So, what commitment will you make to yourself? Will you remain afraid of the unknown? Or, will you take a leap of faith and trust your heart and soul to guide you every step of the way? Your time here is too short to hide your true feelings and give up on what you care about, so go ahead, live boldly in pursuit of your dream, and watch as your life transforms before your eyes.

*****

Every day that you delay doing what is inside your heart is a day you could be working towards the life you dream of. So, it's time to stop believing that it doesn't matter if you pursue your purpose: it does. The calling you feel inside you and that picture of your future you keep wishing were true is not a pipe dream. It's not crazy. It's your destiny. It's what you were born for. And, when you give your whole self to it, all that you have been searching for will find its way right into your life.

That's it. That's the great secret to an extraordinary life, one in which your purpose is the centrepiece and where you live and work with heartfelt vision. Go forth and be yourself in the most magnificent way possible. There's a huge world waiting for you.

PART 2
WEALTH

5

Great Riches Await You

"Wealth is the ability to fully experience life."

Henry David Thoreau

A prosperous relationship with money is essential if we are going to flourish while fulfilling our purpose on Earth. If we hold back from earning and creating financial wealth, then our journey will be a constant struggle of trying to get by, instead of accepting the many blessings that can come our way. And so, it is time to take down the walls between you and the life you desire by deciding that you are ready to thrive on every level and in every way possible, including financially.

Money is a resource with endless possibilities. It can make all manner of dreams and goals come true. Despite this, so few people have a rewarding relationship with it. Instead, their relationship with money is full of lack, limit, and stress. This limits the quality of the life they live and, in some cases, causes them to abandon the dream inside their heart completely.

It doesn't have to be this way. Money can serve rather than stop you. Money can support you in fulfilling your highest purpose. And even though only a small percentage of the population succeed in this area, you can become part of the minority and thrive, which is precisely what you deserve.

Money is all Around You

Regardless of where you are financially today, you are experiencing just a tiny fraction of what is possible for you. One of the reasons for this is that you perhaps haven't realised that money is all around you. Instead of focusing on the many ways you could increase your income - and on the incredible potential you have for wealth - you keep focusing on your own bank balance and the reasons you think you are stuck financially.

This limited perspective on money is exactly what limits your cash flow and prevents you from breaking through your financial glass ceiling. But, when you realise that money truly is all around you, you will be set free from a reality where cash and a lack of it always seem to go hand-in-hand.

You may not know this, but approximately five trillion dollars changes hands around the globe every single day. Take a moment to comprehend this fact and try to picture the sheer quantity in your mind. It is astounding; breathtaking even. When I first heard that number, my jaw dropped and my perspective on money and the world we live in was forever altered.

I began to watch the financial transactions taking place all around me: money being transferred, loans being granted, rent being paid, holidays being booked, debts being cleared, friends repaying favours, houses being sold, people investing in education, and funds being donated to charity. In doing this, I realised that, just like you, I am surrounded by money.

It is mind-blowing to think of the sheer volume of money that changes hands globally on any given day. It's happening as you read this book. One second passes and $100 million changes hands. Another minute passes and someone signs a contract for $250,000. Another day passes, and this time $540 million moves from one bank account to another. Billions and billions of dollars are dancing their way around the planet every day. Wealth permeates the globe. It is awe-inspiring.

Being well-off financially is an essential part of living an extraordinary life, and when you comprehend this on the deepest level possible, you can shake off any long-held ideas that money is absent, scarce, or lacking when the truth is anything but that. It is in cold hard cash, loaded onto cards, stored in banks, invested in dreams, and sitting in an account or under a bed waiting for a rainy day. The magnitude of the global economy is almost unfathomable, and in some sense, this makes money as omnipresent as the air we breathe.

If you think beyond your bank balance for a moment, you will remember that, right now, there are people who have money problems that make yours look like a walk in the park. There are people in developing countries who earn a mere fraction of what you do while working far longer and harder as they fight desperately to survive.

There are millions of people who don't have clean water, electricity, or a roof over their head at night and who won't eat today. As I found out when I travelled to China, there are thousands of people living in Beijing who have never seen the Great Wall of China due to their economic status and circumstance, even though they live just an hour's drive away.

What does this mean for you? It means that even if you have an outstanding mortgage on your house, you are still miles ahead of the people who don't have the option to buy a home. It means that even if you haven't finished paying off your debts, you are still better off than the majority of the human population. It means that even if you are a long way from where you would love to be, you have opportunities that are out of reach for many, and this is something to be enormously thankful for.

Now, I have a question for you: if there truly is no lack of money in the world, then where does the idea that there isn't enough to go around come from? The answer is that it exists only inside our mind. At any given moment in time, you hold ideas about the income you think is too small or excessive, what you think is cheap or expensive, and how much you think you can earn. You have preconceived notions about what is possible for you financially and about the wealth you think you can accumulate in your lifetime.

Somewhere in the middle of these ideas is your money mindset. But here's the thing: these ideas vary greatly from one person to another. Most ideas are based on subjective assumptions, and none of them reflect the whole truth. There *is* no one truth about money that reigns supreme above all others, and whatever you personally believe is true in this moment is precisely what shapes how much money you make and keep.

The key to transforming your experience of money is to understand where your ideas about it originated. Often, our perspective on money is heavily influenced by the relationship our parents had with it and thus, the childhood experiences we had of wealth (or a lack of it). This makes sense as, more often than not, we spend our formative years in our parents' care, listening to the language they used to talk about the family finances and observing how they handled money-related issues.

Maybe you grew up hearing phrases like, "Everything that comes in, goes out," "We can't afford that, honey," or "You have to work hard for every penny." If so, it is possible that these phrases feel as true for you today as they did for your parents when they said them. If your parents believed that rich people are greedy or that money is hard to come by, there is a chance that you will feel guilty pursuing financial goals that far transcend the amount of money your parents earned. If you can relate to this, then this is an internal obstacle you will need to dismantle in order to create wealth for yourself.

On the flip side, if your parents were dedicated to growing businesses and had investing skills, you probably grew up with radically different ideas about money. For example, you might feel that money is easy to make, that there is plenty to go around, and that you can attract and create the wealth you want any time you desire.

Regardless of whether your dominant attitude about money came from your parents or from other financial experiences, it pays (literally) to understand where it was first established. By doing so, you can choose to work on your views of money and set yourself up for a richer future.

We stay where we are financially by becoming too comfortable with the amount we earn, by allowing our income to define our identity, and by following limited attitudes about money that we have adopted from others. We believe that we can't earn more than we already do and that we will be stuck where we are now for the rest of our life. We complain about our current position to other people and the words we speak continue to shape our financial destiny.

Think about it now. What is your running commentary about money? How do you speak about your finances? Telling people that you can't find another $50, $500, or $5,000 for your next goal or repeating that you have no cash is exactly what holds you back from expanding to new levels of income and wealth.

Are you treating money as a limited resource, assuming that there won't be more of it to come? Are you holding on to everything you've got for dear life, acting as if the money you have now is the only money you'll ever make? When you say that you cannot afford what you want, you are unconsciously pushing piles of cash, as well as opportunities to earn it, away from you.

Now, let me ask you this: what would happen if you changed the channel? If you began focusing on the opportunities around you instead of believing that you are confined by imaginary financial walls? If you started believing that you are infinitely resourceful whenever the situation at hand calls for it? If you accepted on the deepest level that money will manifest every time you have a worthy cause for it? Wouldn't that impact your entire experience of life? You would no longer be scraping by just to pay your bills. Instead, you would be in control and living to the fullest.

The wealthiest people I know see money in a different light to the majority of people who struggle with it. They tend to see life as a playground for service, for great achievement, for self-expression, and for making a difference. They live on their terms, not by rules set by people who are less fulfilled and inspired than they are. This perspective is precisely what draws significant amounts of money towards them.

They stand taller, speak clearer, and ask for what they want. They radiate richness, abundance, and possibility to the people around them, which turns them into a magnet for even more money and incredible opportunities. They take their life and financial future into their own hands and craft it into what they wish it to be. This is a far cry from the commonly held viewpoint where people believe their financial situation is anyone's fault but their own.

Small minds believe that money is evil, that those who have it are selfish and greedy, and that if one person becomes richer, another will become poorer. This traps them between their morals around money and their innate desire to flourish financially; a desire that we all have, even if we aren't willing to admit it. Big minds understand how powerful money is and see the many ways it can be used to solve problems and achieve inspiring goals. They are connected to the spirit of wealth and are humble enough to experience it so that they can devote it to a greater purpose.

Choosing your attitude about money matters, because your life will be shaped by how you feel about it and yourself in relation to it. Consider what kind of experiences you want to have. Reflect on where you want to be 10, 20, or 50 years from now. Remember that you hold all the cards when it comes to changing the relationship you have with your finances and determining how your destiny will pan out.

Don't let the world choose how much you will earn. You be the one to choose. Don't just earn what a typical professional in your field is 'supposed' to earn according to history, common beliefs, or popular culture. Instead, be the one who breaks the mould and sets a new precedent for what can be done.

Don't allow people to tell you how to use your money. Instead, be the one who invests it into the goals that matter to you. And last but not least, don't allow what happened yesterday to dictate what you can or cannot achieve today. Instead, be the one who decides how you want your financial future to be, so that this one life that you have is as inspiring and fulfilling as humanly possible.

Be Paid for Your Purpose

There is great power in realising that money is all around you. The main reason for this is that it opens you up to an inspiring possibility for your life: the possibility of being paid for your purpose. Imagine it for a moment. Imagine making money from your talents. Imagine not only being paid to do a job that you love so deeply that you would do it for free but earning your entire living from it. Imagine what it would feel like to be rewarded financially for what comes naturally to you.

This would end the struggle so many people face: the separation between what they love to do and what they are paid to do. Too often, people compartmentalise their finances and their dreams, believing that their source of income must be different from what interests and inspires them. But what if you considered, even for a brief moment, that it is possible to unite the two? What could happen then? The quality, meaning, and inspiration of your life would skyrocket.

I clearly remember the moment I discovered that I could earn an income doing what I love to do. I was just 19 years old and had recently attended The Breakthrough Experience® with Dr John Demartini for the first time, after experiencing my rock bottom moment just a few months earlier. I was working in retail, selling books to help fund the courses I was completing with Dr Demartini (part of the divine plan, I am sure).

At the time, I was connected with a global network of entrepreneurs. One of the members, Philip Krieg, had noticed that I had a natural affinity for writing and felt that I could do more with my life. So, he called me while I was at work one day and during our conversation, he asked me, "Did you know that you can get paid to write?"

That was the moment my life changed forever. The world opened up around me, right then and there, and I saw possibilities for myself that I had never considered before. Suddenly, I realised that I didn't have to work for someone else; I could work for myself. I didn't have to grow a career that didn't inspire me; I could instead follow my heart professionally.

I didn't have to show up at 9:00 a.m., five days a week, to build someone else's dream; I could build my own. I felt free. While in many ways, my journey had only just begun, there is no doubt that I would not have the career I do today had Philip not taken the time to notice my gifts and encourage me to dream of a bigger life for myself.

During the same phone call, Philip hired me to write an article about him which was to be published in an entrepreneurial magazine. I was off and running. I began writing content for business owners globally and established a reputation as a professional writer. Just eight months later, I was attending a program with Dr Demartini, when I glimpsed a heartfelt vision of helping him share his work with people, since it had helped me so profoundly the year before.

What happened just half an hour after I saw this vision was astonishing. I learned from a contact who happened to be attending an event in the same hotel that someone was writing a feature article on Dr Demartini. The article was to be published in the same entrepreneur magazine I had written for. I knew that this was my chance to take my career as a writer to the next level: I wanted to write that article.

I approached Dr Demartini at the front of the room and waited patiently to speak with him. I was nervous, but the possibility of working for him overrode my doubts. I explained that I had already written for the magazine and asked him who was writing the feature article. After answering my question, he said, "Why? Do you want to write it?" I replied, "Yes. I believe in your work, and I know I can do a good job."

Dr Demartini's response altered the course of my destiny from that moment forward. He said, "Well, we'll let him write that article, but we are looking for a team of writers to help me produce my books and content. Are you interested in applying?" My jaw dropped.

Because of my courage to honour my vision and put myself forward for work that I longed to do, I had been offered an opportunity that many aspired for. Dr Demartini knew who I was from his events and, as it turned out, had already been inspired by me. But it was in that moment when I took a risk and put myself forwards that he learned that I love to write.

Less than a year later, I was editing the first manuscript of his book, *Inspired Destiny*. I didn't have a degree for the job, and I still don't. I hadn't studied writing at university, and I still haven't. So, 'on paper', I didn't have the necessary qualifications to do the job. But Dr Demartini knew that I could do it, even though I hadn't written a book of my own yet, let alone edit the draft manuscript of a best-selling book for a famous publishing house. Why? Because I didn't just want to do it, I lived to do it. I cared about it so deeply that it felt like a part of my mission to bring inspirational messages to the world.

Working for Dr Demartini empowered me, both as a writer and as a woman, and gave me the courage to continue pursuing my purpose. I soon branded myself as the 'Word Artist', and by age 23, I had been offered the opportunity to write and publish my first book with a publishing house based in New Zealand and Italy.

In the same month the book launched, I was approached by a woman who demanded that I teach her how to write a book. She was convinced that I was the one who would support her to write her manuscript. That was the day that my career as a mentor to aspiring authors began, and I quickly fell into a groove, working with books and their creators.

Private mentoring turned into live events, where I spoke from a stage with one of Australia's leading event companies, and live events turned into online programs. Soon, I was coaching people from Canada, the United States, Ireland, the United Kingdom, and New Zealand. As well as supporting people to share their message on the page, I began delivering mentoring, masterminds, and programs to support people to follow their purpose and build their dream.

Combined with what was then several published books of my own, I had tapped into not just one but many ways to be paid to do what I love. There is no doubt that this is one of the greatest blessings of my life today, and this is what I want for you.

Right now, you might be thinking that it isn't possible to excel financially doing what you love. Or maybe you know what you want to spend your life doing but you can't see how you can earn money from it. If this is true, then what I will say is this: love yourself enough that you are willing to be paid to be YOU. Believe in your calling so deeply that you allow your work, your purpose, and your source of income to become one. And then, be endlessly creative and persistent in turning what you love doing into a living.

It's unlikely that you will start making big bucks on the first day that you offer what you do to people. This is no reason not to try. In almost every success story you will hear, from famous celebrities, actors, and authors to investors and billionaires, you will see that they started out small and worked their way up. Their love of their work kept them going until they touched the world with their gift and made a fortune in the process. Humble beginnings lead to great endings, but you need the courage to start in order to reach the peak.

I earned $150 in my first writing job. It didn't buy me a ticket to Rome, but it was a start. It was my start. I now had proof that I could be paid to do what I wanted to do. I was equal parts curious and enthusiastic about where it could go, but even more than this, I was grateful for the chance to do something I loved for money.

It was less than a year later that I was working with Dr Demartini, an opportunity that paid far more than the $150 I had earned on my first gig as a professional writer. I generated hundreds of thousands of dollars in the first decade of my career alone by sharing my inspirational messages, knowledge, and wisdom with people globally. It started small, with one small job, but it grew, and it grew fast.

So, don't be disheartened by a small start when turning your purpose into an income, and don't let it stop you from moving in the direction you want to go. If this path truly is where your heart lies, then I am certain that opportunities for greater income will come your way. All you have to do is keep walking down that path with your mind open. Keep doing what you love every single day, apply yourself, develop your skills, and show up, ready to do your thing. Become so good at what you do that people rave about you and your reputation precedes you.

It is because you love what you do so much and because you see it as your calling, your destiny, and your greatest privilege that you deserve to be paid well for it. Because you are willing to do more than others are for the job and because you are prepared to go further than anyone else to deliver the best work.

Every industry needs people who don't just love what they do but who live for it. Why? Because that's when great change happens, when lives are impacted, when revolutionary ideas are born, and when history is made. If you give it all you've got, it will only be a matter of time before you strike gold and see that earning a living from what you love to do is not impossible.

So, embrace the possibility of no longer dreading work, and start looking forward to the week where you wake up bright and early on a Monday rather than wishing it was Friday. Embrace the possibility that you don't have to spend your life doing work that extinguishes the brightly burning spark within you. And above all, embrace the possibility that in as little as 12 months from now, you could be earning your entire living from what you love to do while changing the world with the brilliance inside your mind and the love inside your heart.

Find a Purpose for Your Profit

Financial wealth enhances our experience of life. It brings with it new possibilities, opportunities, pathways, choices, and options. It lifts the burden from relationships. It dissolves stress from the body. It provides security and certainty. It turns wild ideas into reality. It funds legacies and the future we most want to create. It is a life-changer.

Take a moment just now to think about the number of decisions you make, and how those decisions are influenced by the amount of money you have at any given point in time. It impacts your choices in the supermarket, the holidays you take, and the clothes you buy. Naturally, the greater our financial resources, the greater our freedom to make inspiring decisions on all of the above.

But here's the thing: saying that you want more money simply because you believe you deserve it (although this is true) or praying to win the lottery isn't what creates lasting wealth. It's heartfelt vision that does. Millions of dollars won't suddenly be given to someone who wastes it on random purchases and, even if it is, it won't stay with that person for long. But significant financial contribution, opportunity, and funding will keep appearing for those who have connected with a meaningful purpose for their profit.

Big bank accounts follow big visions, with no exceptions. If you focus only on personal gain and indulgence, or you are unclear on why you need the money you say you want, you will more than likely stay on the same level you are on now. But, if you stop long enough to look inside your heart and discover what the true purpose of your profit is, you will set yourself on the path to a new and expanded financial reality.

What would earning more money mean for you? What will it enable you to do, achieve, or create? Do you know why you want to double your income or increase your revenue tenfold? Why does it matter greatly for your future and your purpose that you succeed financially? Sit with it. Reflect on it. Feel it. Imagine your life with wealth and then picture it without it. When the vision you see for financial accomplishment moves you on the deepest level, you know you have found it. In fact, the purpose of your profit may be so inspiring that it brings tears to your eyes.

Your reason to expand your wealth must come from your heart. Without a strong drive from within, it will be all too easy to feel defeated when you come up against a challenge, tax bills and investing shortfalls included. As a result, your finances will continue to reflect your half-in-half-out commitment to creating a fortune of your own. But the day you discover how and why becoming rich matters so much? That will be the day greater profits will start coming your way.

Put simply: money can't show up without you placing an order for it first. How can it? You can't even begin to plan for it without knowing where you are heading. Setting meaningful financial goals for your future is what tells life that you are serious about expanding your wealth. Your clarity about what you want and why you want it will begin to draw ideas and opportunities towards you and, with that, will come more money in your bank account. This won't happen if we pull random numbers out of the air that sound good but have no personal relevance to us. As an author I mentored, Melanie Young, stated, "You don't need it until you need it."

Let's say that your goal is to achieve financial freedom. That is, to have more money coming in from passive investments than your active work in a job or business. Like with all other goals, you will need to know the numbers required to achieve it. What type of lifestyle would you love to have? What does it cost? What percentage does your investment portfolio need to be earning from what amount to provide that life?

It is only when you know your numbers that you can aim for what you want, so write them down for each of your aspirations until they are so clear that you can see the money in your bank account. Dream. Imagine. Decide. Plan. And then act on it. Bring it to life.

Without a purpose for your profit, you will float in a financial abyss where you are sometimes up and sometimes down, but you never really go anywhere. Time will tick by, but you will stay in the same place. The longer you put off choosing a target that inspires you, the longer you will remain caught in a survival trap with money.

How can you be who you are and do your best work on the planet if you are focused on just getting by? Likewise, how can you think about leaving a legacy if all you are focused on is making it through the next day? Until you yearn for the enrichment that financial wealth can bring to you and your life, you won't get into motion and create it for yourself. You need your why so that you can fly.

We are far more capable of earning money and building wealth than we realise, and the moment you set your sights on a goal you care about, you will begin to move towards it. You will find strength you didn't know you had, creative solutions to problems, a work ethic that is bound to produce results, and an unstoppable energy that pulls your outcome towards you.

This is true for every human being, and it is true for you. Ultimately, the depth of your vision is everything. So, focus on forming a personal and meaningful relationship with the profit you desire, one that is full of heart, and choose the bullseye you are going to aim for, because you can't score without goals.

Once you have discovered the purpose for your profit, there is one more question to answer: what will you do once you have achieved your goals? People are often so focused on money as the end destination that they don't realise that it is just a part of a much bigger journey: the journey of life. They may have found a purpose for their profit, but not the purpose beyond their profit, which is where the deepest inspiration for contribution and wealth-building exists.

Human beings are hard-wired to find and fulfil their purpose. Therefore, if you feel disconnected from or are unclear about yours, then making or having more money won't solve that problem (even if finance interests you, there is a likelihood that your reason to master it will still be about something other than the actual money). In fact, earning money without meaning might amplify the issue. There are many people who have riches and yet their life feels empty. So, when deciding on your financial future, bring your life goals into focus first and then let your money goals follow.

It wasn't until my mid-twenties that I developed an interest in building financial wealth. Before that, I wanted money for the occasional shopping spree, my lifestyle costs, repayments on courses I had invested in, and travel (I spent half my income on flights for three years running). I had saved a few thousand dollars here and there and dipped into it at times for various reasons.

I was doing well for someone under the age of 30, but it was only after an extreme challenge that I realised why building wealth mattered greatly. When I reflected on it, I realised that the reasons I wanted to accomplish financial freedom were far more compelling than my desire for a new pair of shoes. They were related to who I wanted to be and what I felt I was born to do.

I saw how financial independence would enable me to focus on what mattered the most. I noticed how, when my money dipped, I sometimes pushed my writing to the side. This, of course, was not something I wanted to make a habit out of, as I am certain that we were all born to do more than work a job we dislike just to pay bills, keep the lights on, and make sure the fridge is full. I saw how I could make my dream come true and contribute to the lives of those I cared for along the way.

The more money I had, the more present I was with the people I loved because I wasn't distracted by an urgent need for cash. I realised that I was of higher service to humanity when I wasn't consumed by worrying about my well-being and was instead devoting myself fearlessly to what my heart yearned to do. And above all, I saw how I could be an even greater inspiration by living by example and showing people that it is possible to build wealth and achieve financial independence while sharing your innate gifts with humanity. That is the purpose of my profit. What is yours?

*****

There is something in this world that you care about with your whole heart. It is the difference only you can make. It is the reason that your life on Earth matters so much and the reason that claiming your wealth is so important; to make sure that you fulfil upon the calling within you.

Money is waiting for you to give it a higher purpose and you need it to help you reach the peak. So, open your heart to it. Let it enter your life. Imagine having far more than you need to survive. Dream of that future; one where you thrive in all possible ways and set your financial wealth in motion.

6

You Are Worthy of Wealth

"When you value you, the world values you."

Dr John Demartini

Money provides us with an opportunity more powerful than anything we would do if it suddenly became an unlimited resource and we could use in any way that we wanted. It provides us with the opportunity to develop the most important relationship in our life: the relationship with ourselves. In fact, the journey to increase our income, find a job we love, grow a heartfelt business, and achieve financial independence teaches us many of the greatest lessons we will ever learn about who we are.

It teaches us what matters the most to us by showing us what we are willing to work for. It shows us how persistent, resourceful, and creative we can be when we apply ourselves to a goal that has deep and personal meaning to us. It mirrors how we feel about who we are as well as how we value ourselves. Thus, the ultimate lesson is not what happens in the moments when we break through and earn our fortune, but rather in what we are required to realise for these breakthroughs to happen: that we are worthy of wealth of every kind.

Love Yourself and Your Money

The way to make anything flourish is to give it love in the form of time, energy, effort, and undivided attention. This includes the financial area of your life. Your money needs your tender loving care if it is going to look after you one day. This means knowing what comes into and goes out of your bank accounts each month, structuring and streamlining your cash flow, and making a plan for how you will use it in the future. Doing this demonstrates your appreciation for money and the many rewards and opportunities it brings.

If you push your money away, money will be pushed away from you. However, if you show up for your money, more money will start showing up for you; but you must love yourself first for this to happen. The more we love ourselves for all that we are, the more love we tend to devote to our finances, and the more they grow as a result. Therefore, it is an expression of self-respect, self-love, and self-worth to manage your money well; to ensure that nothing you earn goes to waste and that your money is put to work to help you fulfil your purpose on Earth.

If you haven't yet begun to do this for yourself, to organise your money so that it works for you, then I want to ask you these questions: why are you withholding that love from yourself? What is stopping you? Why are you putting it off? What is in the way of you accepting the financial destiny that you know is possible for you?

If you want to know how deep and expansive your love for yourself is, complete an honest assessment of your life today. Are you inspired by where you live? Does your partner treat you with respect and appreciation? Are your social circles overflowing with people who genuinely care about you? If you own a business, are you paying yourself well or are you sacrificing everything just to keep the doors open?

Are you shrinking your dreams to match your bank balance? Eating junk food because it is the cheaper option? Booking the budget hotel without at least considering the one you really want? Skipping the wellness treatments your body needs? The answers to these questions reveal all, and in most cases, they show us that we think far too little of ourselves and that there is a great deal of room for growth when it comes to how freely our self-love flows.

The depth of the appreciation you feel for who you are doesn't just define how big your payday and investment portfolio are. It shapes every single aspect of the life you live. It impacts how far you go in your career. It affects whether or not you put yourself forward for that chance to share who you are and what you do with more people. It influences the type of intimate partner you attract and the relationships you find yourself in. It determines the clothes that you wear, the way that you walk, and the way that you talk. It defines how inspired you feel on a daily basis.

Put simply, if you do not love yourself openly without restriction, you will hold the financial area of your life back. In fact, you will hold back your life as a whole. If you keep withholding deep and unconditional love from yourself, money issues will be in your face every day. You will run into financial stress at every turn, struggle to get ahead, and find yourself awake late at night worrying about how you are going to make it through the month. It's no way to live, to go through life barely surviving, especially when so much is available for you once you drop the grudge you've been holding against yourself and start creating what you want.

What is it that holds our self-worth, and thus our finances, back from flowing abundantly? It's the long list of ways you think you fell short in the past. It's the reasons you think you are inferior compared to such-and-such or why you believe that so-and-so is more capable of earning millions than you. And, above all, it's the story you keep telling yourself that you are worth little or can only earn so much.

If you never question that story, if you never try to see yourself as rich, as a multi-millionaire, or as part of the 1% of people who have achieved financial independence, then you will keep accepting crumbs and your dreams of wealth will remain unfulfilled. To say that you deserve enormous riches and a life filled with extraordinary experiences is an understatement, but for me to say that and for you to believe it are two different things. It is time to stop expecting that you will get what you've always gotten and open up your heart to receive so much more.

The amount of money you have in your possession today is not a reflection of how valuable you are. It only points to how valuable you believe you are. Believing that you are valuable starts with the realisation that there is no one else you would rather be but you. It all starts when you realise that you are far more useful to the people you love and the human race when you are prospering than when you are curled up in a foetal position stressing about paying your rent.

Maybe you have spent your entire life believing that you don't deserve more because someone judged you, rejected you, or told you that you are worthless. But here's the thing: your self-worth is never defined by what someone else says unless you agree with what they say. This means that it is up to you to choose what you are worth and to decide that it is your birthright to experience deep spiritual and material riches.

It's not the economy, a bad turn of luck, your employer, your social circle, or the country you live in that determines your net worth. It's you. You are what stands between where you are and the wealth you dream of. So, it's time to consider that what you think of yourself may not be the truth. It's time to appreciate yourself for everything you have been, everything you are, and everything you will become. It's time to love yourself for each and every thing that you have done, be it yesterday or ten years ago, for it brought you to where you are today and set you up for where you will go tomorrow.

It's time to consider that you may have been wrong. Perhaps you aren't worthless after all. Perhaps you are mistaken in thinking that you are insignificant; perhaps you do matter to more people than you realise. Perhaps you missed the mark and you do have it in you to do something profound in this world. You are worth the love you yearn for, and the most reliable source of that love is deep within you, as no one can know or love you the way you can.

Life needs you to move your piece on the chessboard before it can step in and help you. It needs you to make the first move. It needs you to decide that you want more - and not just a little bit more, but so much more - and to believe with an unshakeable conviction that you deserve everything you dream of. It will help you create wealth for yourself by showing you what the next step is; I can promise you this. But first, you need to see yourself as worthy of that wealth. Otherwise, no matter what help shows up, you will either turn it down, push it away, or miss it completely, even if it is right in front of you.

It's time to stop passing on profitable opportunities, giving up on what you want, and pushing your wealth away from you. The power is in your hands to change the way you see yourself and accept the money you deserve. So, take down the walls that you have built around you and bury the hatchet. For when you are truly done believing that you are worthless, both you and your finances will start to bloom.

Earn What You Are Worth

Across the world today, there's not just one person but many people earning a fortune doing what you would love to do. There are singers earning millions sharing their voice and music with people all over the globe. Business owners are taking time out to be with their families or start their next venture because their company runs like a well-oiled machine.

Many financial investors have never worked a nine-to-five job because their portfolio reaps dividends year in and year out. There are chefs who have established million-dollar brands and product lines, personal trainers who are making a mint helping people to tone up, professional speakers who are being paid thousands for each speech, and writers who earn six-figure incomes from their published works.

As you can see, there is an abundance of people who are prospering from their purpose. It's happening as you read this, and there is no reason you can't do it too. Ask yourself: what is the difference between them and you? What is it that enables them to be highly paid for their calling? Do they have a more extensive track record than you? If so, you can develop your experience. Are they more skilled than you? If so, you can develop your abilities.

Have they teamed up with the right people to help them reach new levels in their career? If this is the case, you can find your team. Have they packaged what they do so they can offer it to thousands of people? If so, you can do this with your gifts. Or is it simply that they believe in themselves more than you believe in yourself, and this is why their income is two or ten times more than yours?

We do not differ from one another in our level of income because one human life is worth more to this planet than another. This is far from the truth. We are equally precious, and each of us is born with a gift to share. No, we are separated in levels of income because of the ideas we hold about how valuable we think we are to humanity. And so, the amount of money you have right now is a reflection of your perception of how much you and your life matter to this world.

Therefore, the possibility of earning a fortune from pursuing one's purpose is not just limited to the few; it is possible for anyone. Yet, more often than not, people settle for jobs where they earn a tiny fraction of what they are capable of. Sometimes we earn less than what we desire by staying in a low-level role for the sake of security. Sometimes it is because we are hiding out in our workplace, afraid to ask for the promotion we want.

Sometimes it is because we are offering our services to people far too cheaply or under-pricing the products we sell in our businesses. Sometimes it is because we are underpaying ourselves from the money we earn. Sometimes it is because we have been too afraid to pursue the career of our dreams. And sometimes, it is because we are so busy taking care of everyone else that we forget to take care of numero uno: ourselves. Regardless of the reason, the cost of living your life with a limited pay cheque is one too great to bear.

In my mid-twenties, I changed financial structures from being a sole trader to owning a company. After I opened the business, I devoted all of my time and attention to my work. I spent seven days a week hiring and training new team members, working with clients, managing finances, and constantly pushing the business forward, and all the while keeping my mission to inspire people at the forefront of my mind. As a result of my relentless hard work, I banked six figures in the first six months of opening the company.

Cracks started to show nine months into the first year. I was beginning to feel the impact of the discrepancy between my work output, which had risen dramatically, and what I paid myself in return. I was barely paying myself for my immense effort and devotion, even though I was banking five figures every month. I can recall several moments where my personal debit card was declined at the service station or in the supermarket - not my fondest memories, as you can imagine.

Just 18 months after opening the company and grossing just shy of a quarter of a million dollars, I received a company tax bill that exceeded the amount I had in savings at the time. Layered on top of a burned-out body, it was too much for me to handle. I fell apart. I began withdrawing from the world in an attempt to rebuild my dignity. I paid out most of what I earned in the following year to recover my wealth. I felt like I had failed. I had worked harder than ever serving people, and yet I was in the worst financial position of my life.

The road to my financial and physical recovery was a long one. Looking back today, I am immensely thankful for the loved ones who stood by me when I wanted to throw in the towel completely. But even though those years were without a doubt the toughest I had encountered, it was then that I learned the most powerful lesson of all, which was the importance of paying myself first and rewarding myself for the work that I do.

It seemed that my desire to inspire people, combined with my powerhouse work ethic, had gotten the better of me. This was mostly because I hadn't been willing to admit that, while I wholeheartedly loved what I was doing, I also needed to think about the importance money played in my well-being. The financial breakdown provided me with the opportunity to finally admit that I wanted and needed to be well taken care of and that I was as important as the people I was serving.

Why am I sharing this story with you? Simply because I don't want you to face a financial rock bottom so challenging that it nearly knocks you out of the game, just because you didn't prioritise yourself along the way. I don't want you to pour your love into what you do without also pouring an equal amount of that love back into your own life and bank account. Even though I can count an unlimited number of blessings from this steep learning curve today, I don't ever want money to become an obstacle to your dream.

It is crucial that you stop discounting your services just to get by, that you quit underselling the value of what you do, and that you aim for far more than a minimum wage. If you don't, there will be a compounding impact on you in the long run, from your physical health to your achievements. You will feel burned out and stretched too thin, forget why you started on your path in the first place, or even lose your love of what you do.

The quality of your work will start to drop, and your results will eventually crash through the floor, as you find yourself crumbling on a personal level. It will become increasingly difficult to show up for the world around you if things aren't well in the world within you. So, if my story struck a chord with you, then now is the time to address it. Take it from me: you can't afford to wait. Now is the time to develop deep love, appreciation, and, above all, respect for who you are.

Now is the time to start increasing your personal income. Not tomorrow, next week, next month, or next year. Today. It is time to identify all the ways that you are rescuing other people while sacrificing your own well-being in the process, and it is time to turn it all around. You are here to serve the world, not save the world. So, don't jump into the water in an attempt to bring someone else back to the shore; earn what you are worth and prioritise your wealth.

You are talented, capable, brilliant, and worthy, and you have the power to create a life where you prosper in all ways, including financially. It's what you deserve. You can develop new skills, educate yourself, and put yourself in a position to increase your income, and you can start the journey to do that today.

You've got the goods to go to an entirely new level of income, and if you don't think that you do, you can get them. Skill level and experience need not be a barrier between what you earn today and where you would love to be. In truth, there is nothing in the way of you earning what you are worth. That limit on your earning capacity exists only inside your mind, and you can smash through it anytime you want to.

Maybe the pathway to increase your income is a new job, a different opportunity, a fresh approach to your business, or a giant leap forward towards your dream. Regardless of what the pathway is, you must believe it is possible to expand what you earn in leaps and bounds (and I don't just mean possible, but possible for you specifically). And above all, have the self-worth to make it happen for yourself, so that you can have what you want while being who you are in the world.

Fly First-Class Through Life

The first time I flew first class was a profound experience. I had upgraded my Emirates flight from London to Dubai, and as I boarded the plane, I discovered that, on the A380 airbuses, first class is on the top floor of the plane. This meant that I not only had a cubicle of my own with a mini bar, storage, and an extra mattress for my bed, but that there was a bar in the middle of the plane. Yes, a bar. I enjoyed every moment of being waited on throughout the seven-hour flight (being addressed as Miss Gowor melts me anytime) and, as I disembarked the flight in the United Arab Emirates, I felt inspired.

I spent four hours of the journey working on this very book (it felt appropriate to write about our relationship with money while sitting in a bar flying 36,000 feet above the Earth). As I added content to the manuscript, I had an epiphany: it felt natural to fly first class. Normal, even. And yet, for nearly my whole life, I felt like flying economy was normal and that anything above it was out of the ordinary and out of reach. I believed that travelling in comfort was only for the minority; that the special and extraordinary people were the ones who flew first class and that I belonged in economy class (which stemmed from an assumption that I wasn't special and extraordinary, too).

But when I finally experienced what it was like to be waited on hand and foot, I realised that it was, in fact, the economy class that wasn't normal. I saw how I had been accepting less because I had been seeing myself as less. I saw with astounding clarity how often we do this. That is, we settle for okay instead of extraordinary. We barely dare to aim for what we would love, which pushes wealth of every kind away instead of pulling it right in close to our chest and into our bank accounts.

Why do I share this story about flying first class? Because it is a powerful metaphor for our relationship with wealth. See, most people travel through life with an economy-class mindset. They aim to get by instead of thriving. They assume they can't afford something their heart desires without considering how they could reach it. They are afraid to invest in themselves and in their goals. They are afraid that money won't be there for them when they need it.

A far smaller percentage of people travel through life with a first-class relationship with money. They work for and reach new levels of income and achievement, and they invest and manage their money so that it supports them. They treat themselves to the best where possible and make sure that they are taken care of, so that they can achieve outstanding results.

Reflect on it now. Which mindset have you been flying with? Economy, where it is crowded, the seats are uncomfortable, and you can't get the rest you need? Or, first class, where you have every need catered for, you travel in comfort, and feel refreshed when it counts most?

If you keep thinking that you are poor, you will treat yourself poorly. You will think less of yourself, and never stop to question if perhaps you are worth more. You will live an economy life. But if you believe with every fibre of your being that you are invaluable and that becoming financially free is on the cards for you, then you will find a way to succeed, regardless of the circumstances you find yourself in. You will live a first-class life.

It might require intensive personal development to upgrade your mindset from economy to first class. It might take years of internal reflection to give up the life where you have only what you need while what you want remains on the other side of a glass window. You might need deep healing to realise that how much money you earn and keep has nothing to do with your family heritage, colour, background, race, or religion; that's why there are Slumdog millionaires and people who win the lottery and go bankrupt within a year. But regardless of the effort it takes to upgrade your mindset, it is worth every ounce of effort to do it.

Start seeing yourself as a rich individual whose financial situation just hasn't caught up yet. Stop saying it's fine when it's not. Question what you accept as being enough. Learn to ask, aim, and aspire for more. Realise that financial poverty, while a conscious choice for some, is a reality that most people have sold themselves into, thinking that it is the only way to live.

There may be areas where you consciously choose to spend less money so that you can use your funds for goals that matter more. For example, you might choose a cheaper home so that you can build an investment portfolio or wait longer to buy your dream car because you want to pay off your debt first. I have no issue with decisions like this as they are likely to set you up for a first-class life later on.

The issue occurs when you choose economy options that compromise your well-being. You need a strong personal foundation in order to function and perform in your life, career, and relationships. And so, if you are sleeping on a poor quality mattress that compromises rest, eating unhealthy food that affects your decision-making abilities, or wearing clothes that impact your confidence, it might be time for an upgrade, especially if you are serious about fulfilling your potential in life.

Ask yourself this: is there an area where I am choosing an economy option despite knowing that choosing a first-class one would serve me better? Where am I negotiating on something that I know, deep down, should never be up for negotiation? Flying first-class through life is about knowing what you need in order to feel well, think clearly, and experience a sense of balance that enables you to move forward. And then, it is about becoming religiously devoted to providing that for yourself by choosing higher quality items over those that fall apart easily, reusable instead of disposable, and comfortable over cheap.

If you can't master flying first-class when it comes to the essentials, then how will you ever fulfil your greatest desires including literally flying first-class? So, find the holes, plug them up, and build from there. Decide what your new personal standards are going to be and trust yourself to earn what you need to fulfil them. I guarantee your entire life will be enhanced as a result of your decision to invest in yourself. In fact, you might find yourself wondering why you didn't do it sooner.

One of the biggest learning curves of my journey has been in setting uncomfortably big goals and reaching for them without hesitation. In other words, if I want something that costs $50,000, go and get it. Not being too humble to aim for what we truly desire has been a valuable lesson that I want to pass on to you as it will help you to fly first-class through life. Simply put, it is a lesson about asking for more.

There is nothing wrong with wanting more than you have today. It doesn't mean that you are ungrateful for where you are now if you have your sights set on greater destinations. And, it is not shameful if you don't want to settle for the kind of life someone else is living, regardless of whether that is a parent, partner, colleague, or friend. In fact, bottling up your deepest desires will only make you miserable. So, let them out. A quote I once read is fitting here: "Stop going to the ocean with teaspoons."

No matter what your life might look like today, you are not poor, inferior, or worthless. Wherever you are now is just the circumstance you happen to be in at this point in time. It is just a step on the journey. So, learn to separate how much money you have from your sense of self-worth, because even if you owned the most expensive home in the world, it wouldn't come close to matching even a fraction of what your life is truly worth. And, even when you are a multi-millionaire, your money will just be a scoreboard for what you have achieved and the people whose lives you have touched, and still only a partial reflection of your full value as a human being.

If you keep saying, "It's okay, I don't need much money," or "I'm fine as long as all my bills are covered," then you are leaving the money that could be yours in the hands of other people. You are saying that it is okay to worry about being able to cover your expenses every month and that it is okay to work for decades without being rewarded richly for your dedication. But is that true? Is a life riddled with concerns about your and your loved ones' well-being the one you truly want? Don't you yearn for something more than financial mediocrity?

You will be who you are with or without wealth. But with it, you will be an A-grade version of yourself. You will express yourself authentically, be committed to the causes that move you deeply, and do justice to your God-given gifts. And what emerges from within you when you are no longer consumed by thoughts of survival will be profound. That's why choosing to make a rich life your destiny is so important: because of who you can be, of what you can do, and of the way in which you can change the world once you set yourself on the path to becoming financially free.

For most people, struggle and stress around money is an everyday reality - but it doesn't have to be your reality. Choose not to let your dreams die with the number you see in your bank account. Instead, choose to be one of the people who sets themselves up for fortunes. Do today what will lead you to the wealth you desire tomorrow. Allow the vision of yourself living an inspiring life to move you in the right direction until all your hard work pays off and your money works for you.

*****

The amount of money that you earn in your lifetime is not set in stone the day you are born. That amount is influenced by how deeply you feel that you deserve to thrive financially and how dedicated you are to creating wealth for yourself. It's up to you to shape your experience of money, as nothing can shift your wealth on the outside until you shift your worth on the inside.

Life will push and pull you, serving you a wide variety of experiences until you work out what matters and that one of those things is you. So, make today the day that you design the financial future you want for yourself and decide, with a hand on your heart, that you truly are worthy of wealth.

7

Find Your Financial Power

*"Empty pockets never held anyone back.
Only empty heads and empty hearts can do that."*

Norman Vincent Peale

Our capacity to transform our financial situation is enormous once we realise that the power to create it exists not in advice from financial planners or get-rich-quick schemes, but right here within us. We are not powerless when it comes to creating our fortunes any more than we are victims of what happened yesterday. And so, it is when we start believing that we control money we will have in our bank account tomorrow that we tap into our power to turn our finances around and create exactly what we dream of.

How would you feel if you knew that no matter what happens with your money, you can handle it? What would you do if you knew that financial freedom is within your power and reach? That the capacity for millions is already in your life? And that, if you fall, you have the ability to bounce back, reach higher, and achieve extraordinary goals?

Yes, you are responsible for the place where you stand today, but where you are is far less than what you deserve, and you can alter the course at any time and steer yourself in the direction you choose. You just have to want your financial dreams enough that you will stop at nothing to give yourself the life you desire.

Bouncing Back From a Financial Fall

There is no doubt about it - this might be the heaviest topic in the book. In fact, I almost left it out. But then it hit me: I don't ever want money to be the reason you don't find and fulfil your purpose. Maybe you aren't in a breakdown around money right now, but I write this because I need you to know that you can pull yourself out of a hole should you ever fall into one.

I need you to know it is possible to turn it all around. I need you to know that myself and many other people have done it. And I need you to know that no matter where you are today, your bank balances don't have to be a reason to give up on your dream altogether, which would be a tragic misfortune for both you and the world.

Maybe the money breakdown you experienced happened because of a marketing campaign that failed dismally, a business idea that fell on its face, an inheritance you lost, an unexpected bill, or a breaking point when you realised you were up to your eyeballs in debt. Regardless of how it happened, the first step is to accept it. Is it ideal? No. But will it be this way forever? Not if you change it, which you are 100% capable of doing. While this is how your finances are at this point, it isn't how they will be forever; you are going to make sure of that.

I know what it is like to want to quit because it seems like there is no light at the end of the tunnel, but it's not worth it to give up now - not when the rest of your life is just beginning. I know that you know you can do it, that you can bounce back, and that this is what you want for yourself. And, I know that as much as it might seem that way right now, financial breakdown doesn't have to kill your plans for the future (or your relationship, for that matter, as money pressures often contribute to break-ups).

Focus your mind on a target to aim for. Might the goal seem impossible at first? Yes. Might you sink into a momentary state of depression as you come face to face with 'that number' (you know, the total amount of debt you have, how much you need to pay, what you lost)? Yes. But if you never set the destination, life cannot help you get there.

So, declare what it will be and then stretch that goal far beyond just getting out of the red. Aspire for what you truly want. Focus on what you have always dreamed could be possible for you financially. Doing this will put your current situation in a new perspective so that what previously felt like the end of the world now appears as a mere bump in the road.

You might be picturing a pile of bills in your mind as you read this and thinking, 'How can I afford to think about what I want when I have so many responsibilities?' But let me share something I learned the hard way: don't wait until you're back in the black to aim for the financial future you want. Start now. Aim for the top of the mountain first and then everything else will become just another part of the climb.

If you do this, the gap between where you are and where you want to be will close faster than you can imagine and the path to reach it will show up in front of you. A new idea will pop into your mind, a client or opportunity will drop into your lap, and you will start moving forwards again. You will make progress, pay down that debt, streamline your finances, and bounce back stronger and richer than ever before.

I've heard many stories of people who went from having large amounts of debt to being cash-flow positive and financially free in a short period of time once they picked their target and gave it everything they had. It's time to believe that you will be one of those people, too. You are worth it, and you need to recover fully so that you can fulfil your destiny and show us the greatness you are made of.

Even though it might feel catastrophic, a financial breakdown can be the exact foundation you need to create wealth. It can prompt you to do the things you neglected to do before it all fell apart (such as keeping a close eye on your money). Or it can lead you to do the things you didn't previously have the courage to do, like putting yourself out there in a big way, launching that product, or asking for the help that you need. It might be the impetus you need to start valuing yourself and your money highly. Because of this, a financial fall can be one of the most rewarding experiences you have.

Many of the lessons that help us to create lasting wealth are learned during times where our financial situation is the toughest. For example, you might learn to keep most of what you make, respect yourself, believe in your ability to achieve your goals, connect with the people around you, and set clear targets to aim for. These are all principles that many of the world's wealthy have mastered.

If you don't learn from what happens today, you can't grow to the next level tomorrow. That is true about every area of your life and not just in matters concerning money. So, do what it takes to turn your financial breakdown into a financial education.

Retrace the events that led to the breakdown in the first place. Doing this will better equip you to recover from it and move forward powerfully. You will also realise that, just as there was a series of events that led you to the place you didn't want to be, there is also a set of events you can put in motion to create the outcome you do want. Thus, your wealth is within your control, no matter who or where you are.

The bottom line is that the quicker you learn from your money challenge, the quicker you can move through it. Soon, it won't feel all-consuming. Instead, it will just feel like the training you needed to achieve your goals; training that you can reap benefits from for the rest of your life.

Know this: encountering a financial breakdown in the past doesn't make you unworthy of wealth in the future. That is true no matter how big the breakdown might have been. Furthermore, punishing yourself for how you arrived at this point or kicking yourself while you are already struggling won't help. It will only slow down your journey of bouncing back to a place higher than you've ever been before. So, instead of berating yourself, use that energy to plan for your recovery, focus on your future, and get it done.

Miracles will happen when you decide to work with, not against, yourself, and when you focus on the ways you can fulfil your financial aspirations rather than the ways you think you have failed. The more committed you are to moving on, the faster you will bounce back. So, it's time to let go of the grudge you've been holding against yourself. Truly, it is time.

It doesn't matter if you didn't know yesterday what you know today, because you know it now. Draw the line in the sand, look at yourself in the mirror, and say, "I believe in you." Bet on yourself until you have achieved all your goals. Life is on your side. But more importantly, are you?

I know what it is like to feel as if the sky is falling in on you financially. I know what it is like to work hard and hand over most of what you earn to your creditors. And, I know how stressful it can be to dig yourself out from underneath a pile of expenses. But I also know what is possible if you stay focused on turning the financial tide. I've seen what happens when you take the initiative to set up systems, spreadsheets, and strategies that get the ball rolling in the direction you want it to go.

It doesn't matter where you are in your journey, it is only quarter time in the game. And so, it's not worth benching yourself for a few stumbles that happened days, weeks, months, or years ago, no matter how extreme or challenging the circumstance might have been. You can change your life dramatically if you know what you want - and you want it with enough vigour - and I'll be cheering you on as you go after it.

Step Off the Financial Rollercoaster

If you took the time to follow the financial journey most people take throughout their life, you would more than likely see a peak-and-trough trend that resembles a rollercoaster. Some people's journey with money would mirror the gentle rides that you take with a five-year-old child at the local carnival, and others would look like the monster rollercoaster only a few dare to try: the kind that is sure to make you scream and even throw up.

But either way, it is highly probable that you would see both extremes: the high moments where you throw your hands up in the air and yell "Woo!" and the low moments where you are heading downhill, sure that you are about to go flying off the rails and die. In my humble opinion, while this may be fun at times, especially for the born adrenalin junkie, rollercoasters are designed for theme parks, not the financial area of your life.

There are two ways you can find yourself riding a money rollercoaster. The first is where your mind follows your money. When your bank balance is flush, you feel rich, and it seems that the cards are being played in your favour. The possibilities appear endless and the world seems to be at your feet. You find yourself spending freely because money feels abundant. Life is grand. But then your bank balance dips, either due to your spending, unexpected expenses, or the fact that the cash you received was more of a one-off payment than an ongoing pay cheque… and you dip along with it.

As your money goes down, you start to feel down. The sense of freedom and enthusiasm you previously experienced decreases, and stress and anxiety take their place. The cycle repeats itself. When your money is up, you are up, and when your money is down, you are down. How you feel on a day-to-day basis wavers with the inevitable ebb-and-flow of your bank account, and your money runs your emotions like a puppet master controlling a puppet.

The second ticket to a financial rollercoaster is where your money mirrors how you feel. When you feel inspired, your finances improve. You start making more money, opportunities for income show up everywhere around you, and it feels like you are taking off financially. But when challenges arrive and you can't see your way past the seemingly insurmountable obstacles in front of you, your finances start to diminish.

Personal breakdown in your relationships, career, business, or health can trigger a breakdown around money. Depending on how extreme the challenge is, this can leave you in a position where you need to build your financial wealth all over again, from the ground up. This inextricable connection between how you feel about your life and the state of your finances begins on the day you start making and managing money and continues until the day you die.

Riding financial peaks and troughs will wear you down over time, as scraping it together every month is a stressful way to live. The urgent need to make more money to get by will distract you from pursuing what is inside your heart, ultimately putting your purpose on hold. Chasing money will cause you to run around in circles, burning yourself out in a desperate attempt to survive, and spinning your wheels as you do.

The impact on your personal fulfilment over the years will be enormous. It is difficult to focus on mastering your life if you are too busy trying to survive the huge financial ups and downs to give it the time and attention it needs. How can you receive fresh ideas if you are too stressed to think clearly? How can you see solutions and strategies for the long-term if you are forever focused on getting through today? It's not worth the consequences to keep swinging from one extreme to another. So, it is time to decide that you will choose a different path; that you will step off the ride and take the stable road to wealth instead.

Recognising that you have been allowing your bank balance to impact how you feel or your emotions to run your money, is the first step. This puts you in the driver's seat of the financial area of your life because now you understand that, while you may experience challenges, your money doesn't have to take a nosedive at the same time. It can continue to grow steadily, no matter what curveball is thrown your way.

The next step is to organise your money. Maybe this means completing a detailed stocktake of your current financial position. Maybe it means deciding where you want to go and how you will get there. Maybe it means filing your tax paperwork. Maybe it means setting up detailed payment schedules and reminders for every bill you pay.

It might mean reviewing your outgoing accounts and trimming unnecessary expenses so that you keep more money in your own pocket. Or, it might mean reassessing the way that you manage your cash-flow to accelerate the achievement of your financial goals. Whatever the expression, all of these activities will create the stability and order you need to move towards the future you want.

You will give yourself an advantage if you choose how to run your money rather than letting your money run you. You can do this. You can save ahead of time for expenses, put your tax aside, pile money up for a rainy day, switch to a better business model, and accumulate funds for that dream purchase. You can gain a deep sense of calm and control by laying out the steps to follow moving forwards; steps that lead you to the place you want to be.

As you organise your finances, you will achieve a greater emotional balance, and not just in relation to your money but to your life as a whole. By understanding what tends to throw you off your centre, you can find your inner strength and resilience. Is it after a relationship break-up that your money sometimes crashes through the floor? Is it self-esteem challenges that cause you to dip into your savings? Is it when a plan doesn't work in your business that you start giving up on your dreams and your finances suffer as a result?

If you allow your experiences to send you spinning, you will have a hard time thinking clearly, let alone thinking ahead, when it comes to building wealth. But, if you learn to handle the bumps in the road, you will have a far smoother ride than if you treat every challenge you face as a case of sink or swim.

So, resolve that you will handle your challenges - including financial ones - differently in the future so that the significant events of your journey don't undermine the wealth you have worked so hard to build. Find another way to comfort yourself when a relationship ends or when things don't turn out the way you planned in your business. Discover the secret remedy that picks you back up when you stumble and put support systems in place for when the pressure is on and you don't know what to do.

A deep connection with your purpose is one of the most powerful forces for stabilising your finances. Actively pursuing your purpose will help you to stay focused on wealth-building, as when you have a clear vision for the future, financial freedom will matter a whole lot more to you. With that vision in mind for how your life can be, you will find the persistence you need to keep stair-stepping your way to the top, as well as the patience to stick with it until you have far more money than you will ever need.

The alternative to a life spent riding a financial rollercoaster is a rich one, and not just literally, where cash and assets are abundant. It is a life where, no matter what happens today, you know that you will be taken care of tomorrow. It is a life where your creative energy increases as your wealth expands. It is a life where you continue to grow as a person while your portfolio grows alongside you. It is a life where you can make your invaluable mark on the planet.

It is also a life where you experience what the true definition of the word 'freedom' in 'financial freedom' is: the freedom to be who you are, do what you love, and make every 24 hours of your existence on Earth worth living. So, don't leave your future up to chance. Step off the financial rollercoaster and take control of your destiny. You deserve so much more than a life where you were too worn down by the fight for survival to rise up and share your gifts with the world.

Your Purpose Cannot be Purchased

The majority of the human population is caught up in the alluring pull of consumerism. Bright shiny objects are everywhere. Advertisements bombard us with promises that we will somehow be better off, more attractive, or 'happier' with a new product, gadget, handbag, car, or lipstick.

Compulsive desires to shop and the thrill of the purchase cause people to use their money to acquire material possessions instead of devoting it to growing a portfolio of cash-positive investments. Put simply, the more money we spend today, the less money we keep and invest for tomorrow. When repeated for years on end, this undermines our efforts to get ahead financially.

Most people indulge in a spending spree the moment money lands in their bank account, and a high percentage live with credit card debt because of their shopping habits. The buzz of buying things eventually wears off, leaving people with minimal financial wealth and unmanageable amounts of debt. This is often accompanied by a growing feeling of apathy, as they are now caught in the trap of working for a pay cheque, spending every cent, and beginning from zero each week. After what may then be decades of work, they have very little to show for it.

The feeling of working hard for years on end without also establishing financial security stings, but this is all on us. More often than not, we have earned enough money, we just haven't kept much of it. However, if we keep doing this, where will we be in one or two decades, let alone at the end of our lives? It's a sobering thought, and the reason why is because both you and I know that the quality of your life is a serious subject.

It matters that you can log into your bank accounts and see money piling up from all the work you have done, or that you can check on your investments at any time and see your portfolio growing. It matters that you can look back over your shoulder and see how far you have come. And it matters that you know that being in a comfortable position with money is 100% on the cards for you.

It is your valuable time and energy that you use to earn the money you are paid. So, isn't it true that the last thing you want is for all of it to end up in other people's hands? And isn't it true that you want the ability to turn every one of your dreams into reality throughout the course of your life, without the restriction that living pay cheque to pay cheque brings? Being conscious when you spend money will enable you to dedicate more of your hard-earned funds for long-term investing. It is your way of saying to yourself, "I work hard, and I will make sure that one day I won't have to if I choose not to."

I spent tens of thousands of dollars on clothes as a young woman before I realised that I was, in part, using shopping as a way of running away from my feelings, from my problems, and worst of all, from myself. In the process of trying to find my beauty in the shops and in what I wore, I was giving my power and my money to the store owners. I was trying to buy what I felt was missing in me, and my plan failed, as nothing I bought could ever take the place of a deep and unconditional appreciation for myself.

What are you searching for when you purchase items? Beauty? Charisma? Power? Leverage? Insight? Validation? The moment we look within ourselves for fulfilment instead of in what we buy, we free ourselves from the pull of consumerism. We discover that the answers we seek, about who we are and what our life means, are right here within us and not in the shops. As we reflect inwardly instead of spending outwardly, we discover the purpose that we crave: the purpose of our life, the purpose that enriches our everyday existence, and the purpose that cannot be purchased, no matter how pretty the item or snazzy the gadget.

No amount of clothes will make a woman feel she is beautiful if she doesn't believe it in her heart, just like putting on a new suit won't suddenly give a man a lasting sense of personal power if he hasn't first embodied that power within himself. Those qualities exist deep inside us, far beyond the world of material possessions.

Therefore, buying bigger, better, and shinier possessions won't solve your problems. In fact, it might make them worse as they will continue to fester while your bank balance declines. Will acquiring nice items enhance your life? Yes, but it won't connect you with your purpose or tell you which step to take next to fulfil your destiny.

We waste money when we spend it without thinking, and since (in most cases) we need to spend our time in order to earn more money, we waste our life away in the process, just so we can have more 'stuff' that doesn't and won't matter in the grand scheme of things. You will gain enormous financial power, not to mention a deep insight into yourself, when you slow down enough to notice not just what you buy, but why you buy it.

Nine times out of ten, what we purchase loses its commercial, financial, and resale value the instant we buy it. This means that to get the full bang for our buck, we need to receive value from the purchase that is equal to or greater than the money we parted with to acquire it. How do we accomplish this? It's simple: know the return on investment you receive from everything that you purchase - and I mean everything, from a plane flight to a household item.

When investing in property, stocks, shares, or bonds, your returns are financial. When you invest in other items, you still receive a return, but it is a return of a different nature; of comfort, warmth, peace of mind, inspiration, or growth.

So, begin to think about the value each product or service will produce and then rate how important those returns are. Think like an investor. Next time you are about to fork over your precious dollars and cents to a company, take a moment to ask yourself why you want this item, what problem it will solve, and why it is worth parting with your money for. The answers to these questions will help you to get what you want instead of wasting money on a whim.

We make weak buying decisions when we are caught up in the moment, but when we take a step back and apply even a little rational logic, we can turn our spending into investments. We raise our standards and look for what we need instead of what a sales assistant pushes onto us. We find the higher quality item instead of the first one we see (think silk shirt instead of polyester that creases every time you move) and we stop throwing our money away on things that we regret buying later.

To achieve this, make sure you purchase when inspiration is present. Ask one question and pay careful attention to the response: 'Does this item inspire me?' The answer will either be 'yes' or 'no'. It won't be a 'maybe'. It either feels like it was made for you or it doesn't. You either cannot wait to wear it, or not at all. You can either see a clear and inspiring vision of yourself using and enjoying this item, or you can't. If you are rationalising it, it's not the right one, so keep looking. You know what moves you, so learn to feel and follow it.

You might have to walk away from a potential purchase for a few moments, a day, or a week to answer the question honestly, but think about it this way: if you only buy what inspires you, then your wardrobe, home, and the spaces you spend your life in will only have inspiration in them. You won't have to look at things, wear things, use things, or look after things that don't enliven you.

So, train yourself not to shop on a high, which often ends up in a low. This will be a big win for you as you will end up sitting in your ivory tower counting your coins later in life. And, you will enjoy the fruits of your labour, appreciating the rewards of quality items with meaning.

Over the years, I have noticed that the most fulfilling moments I experience rarely occur when I purchase something. Rather, they are the moments when I am creating something, serving someone, or experiencing the beauty of the world. They happen when I am pursuing my calling and changing lives. Many have occurred while I walked through a city listening to music with words flowing through my mind. In those moments, I feel whole, radiant, alive, and open to the greatest blessings that life can offer me.

Accumulating possessions isn't where the true magic of your journey lies. As a mentor once said to me, "The Porsche and house, they're just a banana!" What he meant was that while fancy cars and superyachts may enhance our life, they aren't what make our life.

If your life is overflowing with meaning, you will naturally need fewer possessions to satisfy you, because you already feel rich in so many ways. You feel wealthy because of the relationships you have, the work you do, and the moments that make your days matter. You don't need to fill the space with random stuff because that space is already occupied with something far more inspiring than anything that spending beyond your means will ever give you: the soul-quenching satisfaction of expressing who you are and doing what you love every day.

You feel less inclined to hand your money over to someone else (which increases their financial power and lessens yours) and acquire possessions that, when you are honest with yourself, you could live without and wouldn't miss if they were gone tomorrow. Instead of a home full of items you don't need and a life that feels empty on the inside, you will reap the rewards of achieving financial freedom.

Not only this, but you will become connected to the richest source of fulfilment, your purpose on Earth; a kind of fulfilment that is free and available to you every single day if you are willing to break free from consumerism long enough to find it.

*****

I want the same thing for you that you do: a life where financial wealth becomes a reality and money is an abundant resource. I want you to know that you don't have to settle for less than you are capable of earning. I want you to know that what you are paid today does not have to determine what you can be paid tomorrow. And I want you to know that you've got this, no matter what obstacles you face along the way.

By knowing exactly who you are and why you are here in the world, you can dig deep inside yourself and find your financial power. So, go ahead, set a transformation in motion today that forever alters your relationship with money and brings with it all the riches and rewards you deserve.

8

Claim Your Fortunes

"God wants us to prosper financially, to have plenty of money, to fulfil the destiny He has laid out for us."

Joel Osteen

You are equally capable and as worthy of creating financial wealth as any of the millionaires or billionaires who have walked before you, and nothing you can do in your lifetime will change that. No shortcoming, no matter how significant it looks, no decision, no matter how detrimental it first appears, and no failure, no matter how catastrophic it seems, can alter the fact that you can experience financial riches in the future if you choose to.

Life wants you to prosper financially. That's why it keeps giving you chance after chance to turn it all around; it is waiting for you to take one. That's why it keeps sending you an endless stream of ideas on how to earn a fortune serving people; it is waiting for you to choose the one that inspires you and run with it.

That's why it keeps making sure you have enough to get through today; so that you can wake up and move forwards tomorrow. It wants you to ask for, earn, and accept more. It wants money to become a reason you do achieve what your heart yearns for instead of the reason you hold back from your purpose. It's waiting for you to claim your riches and thrive.

Remember: it truly isn't where you are now as you read this that determines how the game will end: it's you who impacts that outcome, who decides what your future will be like in two, five, ten, or forty years from now, and who chooses what the final score on the board will be.

Be in it for More Than the Money

In the first decade of my career, I doubled my revenue several years running. I started out earning $22,000 a year, writing for clients while travelling and blogging my way around the world. I earned just enough to fly to the next destination and pay my way while I was there. After three years of flying on a one-way ticket without a fixed address, I decided it was time to return to Australia, put down roots, and grow my business.

The following year I banked $46,000. The year after that, $96,000. In the first six months of opening my company, I banked six figures, and, in the year that followed, my business generated $249,000 in revenue; more than ten times what I had earned when I first started out as a writer.

During this time of rapid expansion, I wasn't focused on making more money. I was focused on finding bigger and better ways to serve people with my gifts. I was focused on the impact I believed I could make, and on who I dreamed of being. I wanted to touch the world and I genuinely cared about helping people enrich the quality of their lives.

I was fuelled by a soulful mission, not by a desire to lay on a beach tanning my derriere. This mission drove me to grow a team, learn about marketing, and expand my business expertise so I could serve people from all corners of the globe. Everything else, including the rapid rise in my revenue, soon followed.

Without intending to, I had stumbled upon a great secret to a thriving business: being in it for more than the money. In the years that followed, I quickly learned that, during times when I lost touch with the heart of my service, my revenue would drop. My desperation repelled potential customers, and how quickly I could make money disappear when I became too focused on the numbers was a great magic trick.

Sooner rather than later though, life would somehow (and without fail) find a way to remind me of the reason I had founded my business to begin with. Ideal clients and opportunities to earn more money would come flooding back to me. When I obsessed about my top-line revenue, I struggled financially until I remembered that, while money is part of the goal, it is not the primary goal of my work. But, when I focused on leaving a legacy and doing what I loved, customers, career opportunities, and new doorways appeared.

Love and heart are the two most powerful magnets for financial wealth, not to mention the building blocks of an extraordinary life. They draw abundance of all forms towards you with incredible speed and force. So, put simply, if you want to earn more money, be in it for more than the money.

You can do this by loving what you do and by putting your heart into your job, regardless of whether you work for a company or you own a business. More than a decade of serving people has taught me that this trumps effective marketing and sales skills every single time.

When you are in it for more than the money, the magic that will happen will make your jaw drop. Out of nowhere, your business will flourish and you will succeed against all odds. I once had a client sent to me by a woman who had dreamed - yes, dreamed - that she had introduced us to one another. She contacted the lead upon waking the next morning and urged her to connect with me. That kind of marketing can only happen when your purpose and your work are one.

People who attempt get-rich-quick schemes they think will earn them a fortune overnight usually fail or fall short of their goal, if the only reason they are doing it is to get ahead financially. They tend to find that a business model or plan that worked well for someone else doesn't work for them, no matter what they do. Even if the plan does work initially and they start earning five or six figures a month, they often learn that it is not sustainable or fulfilling and can find themselves right back where they started. Therefore, it matters greatly that you are in it for a purpose higher than simply earning an income.

To reach new levels financially, you need to genuinely care about people or something beyond you, be it a cause, project, or problem. This is what takes people beyond a job into a business. Often people are working with only their personal goals in mind. But the people who break free from the rat race and become accomplished entrepreneurs are those who care deeply about the impact they can make. Because of this, they simply can't be hemmed in or limited by working for one person. They need a business that enables them to work with more people, touch more lives, and make their difference.

If you are more focused on what you can get than what you can contribute in your career, you are likely to find yourself stuck, financially and professionally. But if you look inside your heart, find out what you care about, and identify who you want to help and in what way, your career and income will take off. Why? Because that deep devotion to a vision beyond yourself, and a desire to use what is within you to assist others, is precisely what makes businesses take off and money pour in.

If you care, people will feel it, and you will go further in every area of your life; far further than those who haven't yet connected with a cause worth working for. While caring about what you do is certainly not the only key to a profitable career, it is without a doubt a powerful starting point.

If you aren't sure what the greater cause behind your work is yet, start by examining your own life in depth. What challenge have you faced that you feel inspired to help people overcome? What result have you achieved that you would love to support others to accomplish? What issue do you see in the world around you that tugs at your heartstrings? What have you learned that you wish more people knew?

Many successful businesses have emerged from a dream, problem, or interest from the life of the founder. Likewise, the answer you are looking for - the seed for a profitable and purposeful career - exists right under your nose and deep inside your heart. The search to find it is worth the time for introspection and reflection as it will unlock a new level of accomplishment when you do.

Life is continually trying to pull you onto the path that has the greatest meaning and wealth potential for you. Why does it matter so much that you take note of the signs and follow them? Because how you spend your life is far more valuable than any amount of money you can make. You can always go out and make more money, but you cannot get yesterday back. As Warren Buffet, one of the wealthiest men to walk the planet, once said during an interview, "I am one of the richest men in the world. I can buy almost anything, but the one thing I cannot buy is more time."

Spending your days doing something you dislike just to earn money is no way to live. Not only this, but your lack of love for your job will hold you back from earning what you are capable of. But, when you turn what inspires you into a living, you will enjoy the experience of working as much as you do the payment that comes from it. Then, and only then, will you step off the treadmill that billions of people are on; the one where they grin and bear their way through the working week to earn money for the weekend… and then do it all again first thing on Monday morning.

People rarely go down in history for how big their house was, how fast their car was, or how stylish their clothes were. Their names make it into the history books because of the cure they discovered for a life-threatening disease, the invention they designed to make people's lives easier, the way their presence lit up a room and warmed the hearts of millions, or the business they founded to fill a gap in the marketplace.

They are remembered for what they did and for who they were, not what they had. They found their calling and knew that fulfilling their mission was their highest obligation while alive. And they pursued it relentlessly, even if it meant sacrificing or investing enormous amounts of money in the short term to see their life's work through to its greatest manifestation.

In many cases, financial wealth followed their career trajectory and fame, but for those where it didn't? Well, their names and souls live on today because of how deep their surrender to their purpose was. What will you do in this world that will be of equal and great significance? How and for what reason will you stand alongside the long line of inspiring people who have made their dent on civilisation?

The wealth you build is merely a by-product of the way in which you have served and helped humanity. It measures and mirrors the way you have been a blessing in the lives of others. It reflects the relationships you have developed and the depth of those connections. It reflects the way you chose to show up, act, help, and live, as well as how you chose to use what is within you to serve people. And, above all, it reflects the degree to which you have done what you feel you were born to do. So, be in it for more than the money, and wealth of every kind will start pouring into your life.

Invest in Your Future

Saving and investing money is far from a new concept. It has been talked about for generations by financial advisors and teachers, from Napoleon Hill to wealth-building books like *The Richest Man in Babylon*. It is generally accepted that saving and investing is a smart thing to do if you want to get ahead. Yet, an extremely small percentage of people achieve financial independence.

While many people appear to be rich because they live in big houses, wear expensive clothing, and drive fancy cars, material wealth is rarely an accurate reflection of monetary wealth. In fact, if you looked into the finances of the people you assume have made it big, you might discover a line of maxed-out credit cards and million-dollar mortgages. A far smaller percentage of people have been patient and devoted enough to grow investment portfolios that take care of them, and yet the rewards of doing exactly this are immense.

Saving and investing for your future is about allowing yourself to receive more than you give. It is allowing yourself to earn more from your investments than you do from a job you work or from the business you run. And, ultimately, it is about allowing yourself to be supported by yourself, by the world, and by your money.

Sit with that for a moment - the notion of being supported by your money. Isn't that a complete revolution on the relationship most people have with money? Where they feel stressed in pursuit of it or on edge when they think about it, and where it seems like there is never enough to fulfil their needs, wants, and dreams?

That's what saving and investing will help you achieve: a privileged position in life where you have transcended the need to trade your time for money (unless you choose to) and can now channel your precious energy towards more meaningful pursuits. Reaching this position is only possible once you let go of anything and everything that stands between you and the financially prosperous future you keep dreaming of.

To build wealth that takes care of you, give up the idea that you have to work yourself to the bone just to survive, even if your parents did. You were not born to be a slave to anyone, so why be a slave to money? To build wealth, believe on every level that you deserve a future where money is your greatest ally, not the Achilles' heel to your dreams. Isn't this what you want for your life? To build wealth, stop standing in your own way and start looking out for yourself instead.

Nothing else says 'I love you' to yourself more powerfully than a payment you make to your wealth portfolio every single week. It doesn't matter how big or small that payment is. The power lies in the act of putting money towards your future. It is a declaration of both self-respect and your belief in your purpose and potential to invest in your financial future, as your financial future is *your* future.

Sometimes people delay saving and investing because they think they can't afford to do it. They worry that if they take a portion of their money and invest it, they will be left with less money to live on. They worry that they will have to give up something that matters to them today to create financial security for tomorrow. But, although this seems logical - because surely if you take 20 away from 100, you end up with 80 - the truth is the opposite. Money attracts more money, and so every single time we invest, it reaps returns, and it happens immediately, not just in ten or fifteen years when you have achieved financial freedom.

Saving and investing will turn you into a magnet for all the things you want most, including career opportunities and relationships that enrich your life. You will feel a sense of progress and enthusiasm when you watch your portfolio growing every week and you see your hard work paying off.

But in order to experience the abundance of rewards that committing to a financial plan brings, you must have faith in the way the world of money works. Essentially, you must have faith in the fact that actively growing your wealth will draw money and blessings of every kind into your life.

So, understand that while it might feel as though you are losing something in the short term by allocating part of your income to investments, you are actually giving yourself something far greater in the future: a life where financial worries no longer plague your mind and you are free to follow your heart, 24 hours a day.

Therefore, transferring money into your savings and investments each month is much less of a 'taking away' and more of a 'setting aside'. It is caring about yourself enough that you want to pave the way to an amazing future. It is feeling a love for yourself so deep that you are devoted to creating a life tomorrow that is even more meaningful than the one you have today. And it is believing that both you and your life are worth investing in and making sure that the money you earn contributes to what you want.

Imagine knowing that the future you desire most, the one where you fulfil your ultimate purpose and prosper in every way, is not only written in the stars but guaranteed. That is pure inspiration, and it is precisely what is possible if you are willing to stop placing your financial future in the hands of wishful thinking, chance, and luck and start actively investing instead.

Setting yourself up financially will provide you with an extraordinary sense of personal power and fulfilment as it is incredibly satisfying to know that you do not rely on anyone else for your security and desires. Making progress towards your money goals will show you that you have got your back, no matter what happens tomorrow. If you save and invest for your wealth today, you can confidently claim what you want for yourself tomorrow.

You can start investing in your future by investing in the asset with the greatest dividends of all: you. I invested extensively in my personal growth and professional development in the first decade of my career and there is no doubt that it set me up for the future I desired. It taught me essential skills, pushed me to think bigger, taught me about human behaviour, helped me to see the world with open eyes, and prepared me for my dream. The same can happen for you.

So, start investing in yourself and build a strong foundation for your life. Sign up for that class you want to take, read those books you know can help you, and spend time with that mentor who inspires you. Realise that you are an asset, that you are worth betting on, and that it matters that you secure your financial future, because only then can you give yourself the best chance at an extraordinary life.

Remember that your path to financial wealth and independence is your business and yours alone. This isn't about impressing someone else with your portfolio, bragging about your returns, or comparing your portfolio to anyone else's. It is about giving yourself opportunities to advance in your career, educate yourself in your field, work with the best team, and experience as much magic as possible along the way.

You might feel that you are starting from nothing or that you've gone nowhere with saving and investing up to this point in your life. Or, perhaps you already have several decades behind you and you feel like you are trying to buy back lost time. Or, maybe you feel that it's too late in the game for you to turn it all around and set yourself up for financial wealth. If any of this is true for you, then let me say that this moment, right here and now, where you decide that you will master your money is the most important moment in your financial journey

Why? Because if you don't make this decision, one that the majority of people never do, then you will never fulfil your financial dreams. However, you must make this decision today - before you buy your first share or property - not when you already have an abundance of cash and assets.

You don't need a million dollars in the bank or a master's degree in finance to build wealth, and you don't need to be a mathematical genius to make your money work for you. So, take a stand for the wealth you dream of having and start saving and investing. Build what you want for yourself. Remember that the higher intelligence that created you - the source of all human life and the birds and the bees and the trees - wants you to become wealthy so that your precious time, talent, and energy are invested into changing the world instead of worrying about a $30 grocery bill.

Building Wealth Fulfils Your Purpose

It doesn't matter who you are, how much wealth you were born into, or what your background is, you will face money challenges during your life. You might hit rock bottom financially more than once, encounter dramatic dips in cash flow, make decisions that result in a loss of money, or experience recurring doubts and questions about your value and worth as a human being.

Although it might feel like it at times, the obstacles that you face do not mean that you aren't destined for riches; they are part of the journey to get there. And, whether your future is one where you scrape by or one where you have more than enough money ultimately rests on one thing: how strongly you feel that building wealth is non-negotiable.

When you believe to your core that being well-off financially is essential for the fulfilment of your purpose, you will become driven and determined to achieve it. You will be patient and persistent when it counts most, and you won't give up on your long-term goals the minute things get tough. You won't just attract opportunities to expand your wealth, you will actively seek and create them for yourself. You will do what you need to do and stop at nothing on the path to becoming rich.

Maybe you are afraid that if you build wealth for yourself, people will think that you are only in it for the money. Maybe you worry that your family will think that you are greedy for wanting more. Or maybe you are concerned that your partner or your friends will think that you are selfish. If this is you, remember that giving power to people's opinions will only hold you back from achieving your goals.

Here's the thing: it is only the people who haven't set themselves on the path to financial independence who have issues with people who are establishing or have already established riches. I doubt you would hear a billionaire tell a millionaire that they have too much money, or hear a multimillionaire tell a budding entrepreneur that they are aiming too high in their business. Thus, it literally pays to filter out any uninspiring judgements about your financial aspirations, because it's true what they say: you earn the average of the ten people you spend the most time with.

You may be afraid of people thinking you are focused more on earning a fortune than helping people. But the truth is that the very act of having more money than you need is what sets you free to work purely because you love it. In fact, showing up to serve people even though you don't need to for your personal survival will show the world just how deep your devotion to your calling is.

However, if you are showing up because you are desperate for the money, people will feel it. In some cases, it may cloud the purity of what you originally set out to do. But, by growing your financial wealth, you can soon reach a point where, yes, people may know that you have accumulated riches for yourself, but they'll also see you as someone who puts their heart and soul into their work and thus deserves everything they have earned.

Money isn't good, bad, virtuous, or evil. It's a resource with a purpose, just like air, food, and water, and its purpose is to help you express your fullest potential. Do you think air, food, and water are evil? I doubt it. Do you resist them or judge those who have them? No, you know that you need them to survive. They feed and nourish you so that you can get on with the task at hand: living the most fulfilling and inspiring life possible. Money is the same, and starving yourself financially is no more noble than skipping meals to save the starving or trying to hold your breath to give other people more air.

If you keep denying your desire for money, the potential inside you that's waiting to emerge may never see the light of day. Sure, you might make a ripple, but never a big splash. I say, be like the billionaires who have made lasting contributions to humanity through their companies, their donations, and their causes; the ones who have stopped at nothing to leave their legacy on Earth.

How would you feel if your financial survival wasn't at the forefront of your mind? Would you move towards your goals and dreams with greater confidence? Would your belief in yourself grow? If you knew that your money was organised to support you, you would feel that life is on your side. You would care less about other people's opinions of you and feel that anything is possible - because it is. You can't change the past, but you can make this your reality for the future.

You can do far more for the world with financial wealth than you can without it. This doesn't mean that it's impossible to create a splash if you aren't loaded right now. My writing inspired thousands of people in my early twenties, despite the fact that I was earning a low income. But there is no doubt that the more money you have behind you, the better equipped you will be to make your mark on the world.

If you knew that you could create a new product with greater resources, would you be willing to accept more money? If you knew it was the key to touching the lives of the people who need you the most, would you be humble enough to earn a fortune to make it possible? And if you knew that becoming a multi-millionaire would enable you to impact the lives of future generations, would you finally accept your destiny as a wealthy individual?

You can set an extraordinary example for people if you are willing to become rich. When I realised that I could inspire people by growing my wealth, I was sold on the idea of creating financial independence. No longer was I afraid of what people might think about my plans, because the contribution I could make by empowering myself meant more to me than any criticism I might encounter along the way. I saw how investing in my future could show people that we truly are worthy of wealth which, in turn, could give them permission to rise up financially, too.

Don't you prefer to spend time with and learn from people who are well-off rather than those who are struggling their way through life? The latter waste their precious time (and lives) cursing the government, their next-door neighbours, the economy, or their employer for the way things are.

But people who accomplish financial greatness often initiate movements, fund projects and products, innovate solutions, and use their resources to effect change on the planet. They show us that it is possible to make a mint while doing what we love and remind us to never ever settle for less than we are worth. That alone is a priceless gift. So, why not be one of the people who gives that gift to others?

Each person defines financial wealth differently. To some, it's a net worth of billions. To others, it's a property and share portfolio worth millions. And to some, it's having double the amount of money they need to fund the lifestyle they want. What that number is for you will change as you go through life (I remember thinking $10 was a huge amount of money as a child), but regardless of how you define a fortune, it is time to dismantle every wall between you and the money you could be earning, managing, and investing… and accept a whole lot more.

I know to my core that there is a difference you want to make on this planet, and you need resources and wealth behind you to do that in the most extraordinary way. You have bigger fish to fry, and you can't make it if you are struggling financially.

You will touch hundreds, if not thousands or hundreds of thousands, of lives as you pursue your purpose, from the jobs you create to the people you serve. Therefore, it is not a selfish act to make sure your money is taken care of. It's perfectly healthy and is a gift to those around you. So, build financial wealth to ensure that your presence is felt by this world, long before and after you are gone.

*****

A strong relationship with money matters greatly for your future. Money will fund the fulfilment of your purpose, aid the achievement of the goals that inspire you, and support you to do your best work.

Without it, you will go through life stopping, starting, and stressing. But with it, you can build momentum towards your dream and bridge the gap between where you are and where you want to be.

When you are clear on what your purpose is and how money enables you to fulfil it, you will be free to express yourself openly, earn a fortune, and live a life that inspires you daily. This is the stage from which you can be who you are, have what you want, and change the world.

PART 3
WORK

9

Use Your Work to Change the World

"You are not here merely to make a living. You are here in order to enable the world to live more amply, with greater vision, with a finer spirit of hope and achievement. You are here to enrich the world, and you impoverish yourself if you forget the errand."

Woodrow Wilson

The fact that you are reading this book tells me that you know you can do something extraordinary in this world. It tells me that there is something you can do to make a difference for humanity, even if that is in a small yet meaningful way. It tells me that you don't want your work to be something you do for the sake of a pay cheque. And, it tells me that you want a career where, by being exactly who you are and doing exactly what you dream of doing, you make an impact that counts.

It's time to revolutionise your relationship with work so that it becomes so much more than a necessary obligation. It doesn't matter how old you are or how unqualified you might think you are; you can transform your career from going nowhere to going places. You can find flow in your work and experience the deep satisfaction of earning a living from what you love to do. This journey starts by merging your heart with your work, because then, and only then, can you take the world by storm and make your ultimate contribution to the human race.

Merge Your Heart With Your Work

Most people see work as an obligation and, more often than not, something they wish they didn't have to do. They put up a wall between their job, where they go to earn money, and the rest of their life, where they do what they love with the people they love.

They dread going to the office, count down the hours while they are there, and can't wait to leave. This mismatch between what their soul calls them to do and what they are paid to do leads to low performance, a desire to drink coffee and eat sweets to pass the time, and a career and income that flatlines. This is no way to spend the precious years of your life, especially when you remember you only get to live each one once.

I only worked one full-time job, during which I clearly remember feeling that I had no life outside the office. There was a limited window of time each week within which I could do what I enjoyed, which was to study personal development and write. It was 80-20 in favour of my job. Like many people, I was spending my energy and using my skills and ideas to help someone else achieve their career goals while sidelining my own.

Despite having a steady income and bonuses, I lasted just three months in the job before I decided I couldn't ignore the inner knowing that I had so much more potential than to work for a company that wasn't my own. I wanted to do great things, and in my heart, I knew that I was capable of making a bigger difference with my unique gifts.

That's when I realised what work was really about for me and what it can be for each and every one of us: making an impact, and as the title of this book implies, changing the world by being who we are. It is so much more than a source of income. It is a chance to use what is within you to touch the lives of other people and be rewarded for it. It is the ultimate avenue for self-expression, whether that is to stand on stages, toss around business ideas in a boardroom, make breakthroughs in human potential, or create masterpieces in your studio.

It is the opportunity of a lifetime: to contribute to the world and live an extraordinary life while doing so. So, why not make your entire life, including your career, revolve around your highest purpose and spend your time doing deeply inspiring work? That type of work is within me, it is within you, and it is within every single one of us, regardless of age, upbringing, or nationality.

I saw Ludovico Einaudi, the Italian composer and pianist, in concert before writing this book. The energy in the room before the concert even began was electric. Several thousand people were waiting to experience his genius, live and inspired.

Ludovico walked towards the centre of the stage and sat down at the grand piano with his back turned to the audience. After a few moments of resounding silence, he opened the performance with a shortened version of his well-known piece, *Divenire*. The instant his fingertips touched the keys and he played the first note, tears spontaneously began running down my face.

The love and inspiration in the room was palpable. You could feel it throughout the entire concert. He expressed himself without words, moving the audience with his music. Every note felt as though it had been written from the very core of him. You could feel his heart in the music; it was tear-jerking. The standing ovation at the close of the concert lasted for at least 15 minutes. It was a humbling and truly powerful experience. I had been in the presence of his inspiring work and the memory of it still moves me today.

Inspiring work is where the soul of the creator can be felt, seen, or heard. It is the type of work that brings out the best in each of us. It is the type of work that merges your dream with your career and your higher calling with how you earn a living. It is where your soul's purpose and what you do every day become one. You feel at home when you do this work. You express, explore, and use all that is within you. Your work becomes a vessel for everything that inspires and intrigues you.

The walls between who you are and the work you do melt away. The writer and the book become one, the business becomes an expression of the founder, the love of the chef can be tasted in the food, the performance and the dancer merge together. Who you are shapes and defines your work, and your work shapes and defines who you are.

This experience of work brings you to life. You pour your heart into what you do. You push yourself to improve, every single day. You wake up with ideas for your projects and can't wait to dive into them. You work for hours on end, long after many others would have stopped.

This great work - this task, this field, this art form that moves you so deeply - beckons to you day and night. It accompanies you through every twist and turn of your journey, never once leaving your side, your heart, or your mind. It holds within it the key to the career you dream of and the opportunities you desire. Every second you pursue that work is a second spent fulfilling the purpose of your life.

What is the work that inspires you most; the work that your soul came to Earth to do? You stay up late and burn the midnight oil to perfect it, it doesn't leave your thoughts, and it inspires your creativity, originality, and genius. If you would get up at 6:00 a.m. on a Sunday morning to do it, you know you have found it. You see a vision for where it can go, and you want to take it to great places. It touches and moves your soul.

That work is the kind you make great sacrifices for, and you are rewarded ten-fold every time you do. You give it everything you have, just to see if you can break through to new levels, and it gives back to you, flooding your life with fulfilment every single day.

If your work feels like a chore, you will wait for it to end instead of being excited for it to begin. You will close your heart off from your profession and go through life disliking the jobs you do. You will underperform at work and watch other people getting ahead while you are scraping by in a career you couldn't care less about. You will never know just how extraordinary your life can be when your soul and your work become one. The tragedy of this is that you won't touch the world the way you and I know that you can nor leave a legacy that will long outlive you.

All great legacies, from billion-dollar businesses and global music careers to remarkable literature, were left by people who poured their heart into their work; people who were courageous enough to let their calling consume them, guide them, and direct their entire life. They allowed it to bring out their innermost talents and they went down in history because they were brave enough to follow their intuition, against all logic and odds. Great legacies are a labour of love from the soul, not a chore assigned by a boss who signs pay cheques. They can only come from the core of who you are.

I declared myself unemployable just a few short years after quitting my last job. While the journey since hasn't always been easy, you couldn't pay me to give up what I do today and work for someone else. It's my dream. All the stumbles, falls, and breakdowns along the way have been worth every effort as, at the end of my life, I will be able to say without a doubt in my mind that I gave it my all. I will be able to say that I never gave up on my calling to inspire people to live a greater life.

As Luciano Pavarotti said, "People think I'm disciplined. It is not discipline. It is devotion. There is a great difference." That is the relationship I want you to have with your work. The one where your work is the pursuit you can't get enough of, where it consumes you in the best of ways, and where what you do is what your entire being is wired to do. If you don't love your work, you won't feel ignited with ambition, nor know the great satisfaction of creating or doing something that expresses who you truly are.

So, set yourself free from work that leaves your greatness untapped, waiting within you to come out. Pursue the career path where you can show up as you are and let your spirit run free doing the work you love: the work that can touch hearts, open minds, and change the way people live. It is the greatest gift you can give to yourself and the people around you, to merge your heart with your work in this way, and when you do, it will take both you and your career to extraordinary places.

You Are Valuable to the World

Let me ask you this: what would you do with your life if you knew that what you have to offer was worth millions? That there are countless people struggling with a problem you know how to solve? That if you offered your gift to the world, people would pay you for it? Would you change career paths? Run your business differently? Create a new program, course, product, or service? Put your hand up for new opportunities?

We all have something of equal value to bring to the table, with no exceptions, and the path to making a meaningful impact is to connect with your purpose, find your unique gift, and share it. My purpose is to write, and my gift is in my ability to touch, move, and inspire people with the written and spoken word. What about you? What do you have within you that you can offer? Which skills, knowledge, and talents have you been downplaying but that you know can set a change in motion in people's lives?

Too often, we take our gift for granted. We don't recognise how valuable the skills, talents, wisdom, and knowledge we have are, nor realise how many people could benefit from them. Because of this, we remain as a 'best kept secret' and we hold back from our dream, afraid that we might not make money - or enough of it - if we pursue our purpose relentlessly. But the more you see and appreciate the value of your gift, the greater the number of people you can serve with it, the further you can go in your career, and the deeper the well of money you can earn from it becomes.

Just because something comes naturally to you does not make it less valuable. On the contrary, this is the exact reason it is so valuable. Just because you love to do it - whether that is to dance, write, paint, cook, build businesses, run, lift weights, or sing - doesn't mean that you cannot or should not earn money from it. In fact, if it's something that you love to do and you have invested countless hours into perfecting your skills, then this in itself is proof that you have stumbled upon your tremendous value to and in the world.

Once you comprehend the power of your gift, it's time to add a monetary value to it. Ask yourself how much what you have to offer is worth and find out how much people would pay to experience it. It doesn't matter if the price tag you place on your gift is small to begin with. It just matters that you start declaring that what you know and what you can do is valuable - valuable enough to earn a living from. If you have the courage to do this, you will see new possibilities for yourself and transform your entire life in the process.

As people pay to experience your inspiring work - your gift - you will see a ripple effect in motion. You will see people being moved by your creations, achieving goals with great meaning, and their lives being changed by your presence. People will thank you for being there for them in tough times, for helping them solve a problem they faced, for sharing your talent, and for showing them what is possible.

Over time, your belief in your abilities will grow, and the opportunities you receive will grow along with it. You will see your value unfolding before your very eyes, happening again and again, until one day you can no longer question whether what you have to offer is worth millions, or even billions, to the human race. These defining moments where you comprehend just how valuable your gift is will help you to stair-step your way to a career where you fulfil your purpose, earn the money you would love, and make even bigger dreams come true.

The deepest comprehension of how essential you are occurs when you look beyond the value of your gift and into the value of who you are as an individual. It is when you realise that your presence alone is a blessing. My mother is an inspiring woman who founded her business, Mama Rae's Soul Food, at the age of 69. Her gift comes largely from six decades of experimenting with food and flavours, as well as a lifetime of research into the fields of spiritual and physical wellness.

She has created a countless number of delicious original recipes. There is no doubt about it; she cooks with love, and each person who enjoys her meals feels that love. But that love doesn't stop with her kitchen creations. It's who she is. Her capacity to see the beauty in people and love them unconditionally humbles me every day, and I have said on more than one occasion that she has enough love inside her to heal a nation.

When she hugs people, she doesn't just embrace their body. She embraces their entire being, mind, and soul. The love she has overflows from her heart to theirs. It helps them to discover who they are, believe in their abilities, and find their way forward in life. It is her presence that makes her so infinitely valuable and, just as it is with you, her gift with food preparation is a fringe benefit. It's her way of expressing that love with humanity. There is no doubt in my mind that she can serve a million or more people and earn the fortune she deserves by sharing who she is with people, and so can you.

Have you ever stopped to reflect on what is so special about you? At your core, do you know without a shadow of a doubt that you are valuable because of your physical presence, your heart, your spark, and your spirit? What do you offer the human race just by being who you are? An open heart? A warm smile? A creative mind? Original ideas? A fresh perspective? A glimmer of hope?

If you saw yourself through the eyes of love for a moment, you would realise just how precious you are. You would start to feel worthy of a far more enriching career and a greater pay cheque than ever before. Perhaps for the very first time, you would see clearly how much your time and energy are worth.

When we comprehend how valuable our presence and gift are, we walk taller, stand with confidence, and speak with purpose. A new grace and poise emerge from within us. We stop selling ourselves out and start betting on ourselves instead, knowing that we cannot fail, and that life will catch us if we stumble.

New ideas for how to merge our soul's purpose and our professional pursuits flow freely to us. We open outwardly, share what is within us, and allow our hearts and our bank accounts to fill up. We draw towards us the people, the magical moments, and the experiences that we seek that make our careers and our lives a rich and extraordinary place to be.

It is one of the great ironies of life that it is often far easier for others to see our value than it is for us to see it ourselves. But if you live every day with a deep-seated faith that you have something within you that you could share with people the world over, you will find it. I guarantee it. It is just a matter of time, but you must believe it to see it - and it is there.

Remember: you were put on this planet with cause, reason, and purpose and your greatest opportunity and responsibility in your lifetime is to do exactly what you were designed by the hand of God to do. As you see and feel with every fibre of your being how valuable you are to the human race, you will know for the rest of your life that an inspiring and fulfilling career is possible for you, and that you truly can use your work to change the world.

Share Your Gift With Humanity

Your gift - the ultimate expression of your greatness - is within you for two reasons. The first is to bring meaning to your journey as you explore and express it. The second is to share it with the people who need it. In order to fulfil your purpose here on Earth, it is vital that you use your gift, as that is how lives are changed, differences are made, and legacies are left. Furthermore, your own life will flourish because of the impact you make with your inspiring work. This simply cannot happen if you keep your talents hidden.

Whether or not you realise it, you have been using your gifts throughout your life. But now, it is time to harness your courage and let many more people know that you exist. It is time to tell them that you are here and that you have something that can help them, whether that is a solution to a problem, an answer to a long-held question, or a work of art that can bring beauty to their lives. It is time to build the bridge between your gift and the people around you so that they can line up at your door to experience the magic of your life-changing work.

The first step that you could take to share your gift with humanity is to complete an apprenticeship. This apprenticeship might be a literal one or a paid project or role of a different nature. Either way, this apprenticeship will prepare you for the next level of your career by providing you with the opportunity to learn from people who are already doing what you dream of doing.

Writing for entrepreneurs early on in my career, including the privileged opportunity to work with several high-profile leaders, was an invaluable apprenticeship for my future as an author. While helping them to fulfil their missions, I acquired essential knowledge and wisdom that prepared me to write for the world. If you are humble enough to learn from masters, you too can become one.

If the first step to share your gift isn't through an apprenticeship, you might choose to focus on finding or creating your dream job. I have met people who found their sweet spot in a job, and maybe you too are one of those rare and fortunate individuals who looks forward to arriving at the office and stays late at night by choice.

Finding your dream job might mean being hired as a chef at the most expensive restaurant in town, being employed to design cars with a leading car manufacturer, or working with the top mentors in your field. Regardless of the form, your job could become the pathway for you to develop your gift and fulfil your purpose simultaneously.

You might make it your goal to move your way up the company you work for, or in another company in the same industry, until you have your ultimate job. If this inspires you, then focus on developing your existing strengths and give your job your all each day. Become outstanding in your field by scaling up the quality of your work until you are at the top.

Might you one day find the desire to step out and create your own company? Yes, and maybe you are already there as you read this. But, in the meantime, you can accumulate experience and ideas while you earn a living doing what you love.

Maybe the ultimate pathway for you to share your gift is to launch a business. Maybe it is to produce programs that allow people to learn from you. Maybe it is to create a line of products that are stocked in stores across the world. Maybe it is to become a highly sought-after speaker who shares inspiring messages and valuable content with audiences globally. Maybe it is to offer services that help people to heal their body or plan their financial future. Or maybe it is to establish a multi-million dollar brand, for example, being a famous athlete or musician.

Regardless of what the pathway looks like, the goal is the same: to make your difference by expressing yourself the way life intended you to. Then your work will no longer be a place where you put your dream on hold. Instead, it will be a place where you share the brilliant essence of who you are. It will become a playground to experiment in, a platform to dance on, and a space where you feel the most at home and alive.

The fear of failing as you move towards a career that inspires you might be slowing you down. What if you go backwards financially? How are you going to explain your plans to your family? What if you give it your all and it isn't enough? Maybe these thoughts are running through your mind right now: 'The world won't accept me for who I am; no one will want to listen to me; I don't want people to find out _____ (fill in the blank) about me; other people do it better than me; people will reject my message, product, idea, service.'

But here's the thing: if you don't move forward, you won't go anywhere, and succeeding in life requires taking risks. Sometimes it requires small risks, like scheduling in time to work on your music or your business, and sometimes it requires big risks, like telling your partner that you have decided to leave your job behind and open a business. In both cases, you will need faith in spades.

The moments where you feel the most afraid of failing are the ultimate test of how much this path you are on feels like your destiny. They provide you with the opportunity to strengthen your faith in your gift and to believe in yourself deeply enough that, regardless of what happens, you can pick yourself up and keep going. They give you the chance to find out whether you have unshakeable certainty that this thing that you love to do so much is what you were born and destined to do.

The key to navigating your way through the fear of failure is to keep progressing and continuously strive to improve your work. If you never try, you will never know where your strengths lie, and if you never push yourself to the edge, you will never figure out that you can fly. It's where all the growth and rewards you seek exist. Know that a life spent in pursuit of your purpose where you come up short, again and again, is still far richer than a life spent hesitating, too afraid to step up to the plate and give it your best shot.

You might not realise this, but the people whose lives you can touch are looking for you. There are hundreds, thousands, tens of thousands, or even millions of them waiting for what you have to offer, for what you are working on, for what you can't wait to share. Can you picture them in your mind? Do you know who they are? Can you feel their presence?

They want to see you dance across the stage, hear you on the radio, watch you perform a miracle in their business, attend your workshops, sit at your feet and learn from you, admire your art, listen to your music, or read your writing. If you don't step forward, they will miss out on your gift. The people who need healing will keep suffering. The people struggling with a problem will keep battling. The people who need inspiration will remain uninspired. That's how important it is, how much it matters, that you let your talents flow freely.

You don't need to be everything to everyone or try to produce or do something that every single human being wants. That would be an impossible feat. You weren't born to do everything, but you were born to do *something*, so focus on doing that one thing for the people who love it, who can't get enough of it, who rave about it, who appreciate it, and who love you for it. That is where your biggest impact will be made, where your presence will be felt, and where your footprints will be left in the sand.

When you boldly put yourself out there, life will start opening doors for you. As you courageously express who you are, the right people will resonate with you. As you show up ready and willing to serve, people will show up ready and willing to be served. As you contribute your special kind of magic, magic will start showing up all around you. As you share your gift with the world will start sharing its gifts with you.

So, no matter how afraid you might currently feel of revealing your unique and precious gift, don't give up. Harness your courage every day to meet humanity halfway and offer what you have. Focus on the problems you can solve, the value you can provide, and the people you can help, instead of all the reasons you might not make it big. Pick yourself up when you fall, keep at it when you think you won't make it and, as Charles Bukowski said, "Drink from the well of yourself and begin again."

It might seem that the time is never quite right to start sharing what you can do with more people, but the truth is that it is always the right time. You are here with a gift you can express, and your life, just as it is right here and now, is the stage from which you can begin that journey. It is from this moment that you can move forwards with courage and confidence, being who you were born to be and doing what you were born to do.

Picture yourself touching the lives of thousands globally. Envision people flocking to you to experience what you can do and what you have created. Imagine the extraordinary experiences you could have in your career, from heart-warming testimonials and achievements to moments when you are acknowledged for the lives you have changed. Don't ever give up on sharing your gift with people because this work you cannot wait to do is not only important, it is your destiny - the very reason for which you were born.

*****

Your love is the greatest force you have for healing, for changing the world, for giving hope, for achieving results, for creativity and breakthroughs. So, merge your heart with your work. Pour your love into what you do and do what you love, every single day, without fail. Focus on the great and worthy work you would love to spend your life doing. Then, devote yourself to it.

As you do, you will not only discover all that you are capable of doing and being, you will also transform your life to the point where you can say that you are grateful for each and every moment of it. At the end of your years, you will have left the most inspiring legacy possible: the legacy that lives inside your heart.

10

Grow the Career of Your Dreams

"Whatever you can do, or dream you can, begin it.
Boldness has genius and power and magic in it."

Johann Wolfgang von Goethe

If you had told me when I was a teenager that I would become a full-time author, speaker, and mentor inspiring people to fulfil their dreams, I would have questioned whether it was possible. It would have been a stretch of my imagination to believe that I could earn six-figure incomes working with people from all corners of the globe. It would have felt like a far cry from the $14-per-hour retail job I worked at the time. But see, this is what happens when you decide to devote your profession to your purpose: you can grow the career of your dreams.

Knowing what you love to do and the difference that you can make for people is undeniably the starting point of an exceptional career as it will show you which direction you want to go in. But then? It's up to you to dive in with both feet. To give your dream everything you have and more. To put your heart on the line, time and time again, and do whatever it takes to make that career a reality. And finally, to stop at nothing as you align your work, purpose, and income so that you can fulfil the highest reason for your existence on Earth.

There Is Room for You at the Top

It's easy to look at the world around you and think that there is no room for you at the top. To look at the leaders, the top performers, and the high achievers in your industry and think that the world doesn't need another one; that the spots have already been filled. Or to look at well-known celebrities and assume that you can't be one of them, too. Or to see the best-selling books in the genre you want to write for and think that there isn't space on the shelves for the one you want to write. Or to watch award-winning movies or hear the top-charted songs and conclude that what you want to produce is irrelevant.

Believing there is no room for you to succeed in your career stems from the assumption that the world does not want or need you and your uniqueness. But what you have to offer matters, and it matters greatly. What you can do matters, and it matters greatly. And who you can be matters, and it matters greatly.

If you stop looking at the top people in your industry and those you consider to be legends for a moment, you will see the countless people around you who can benefit from who you are and what you bring. You will start to see what you can do today to make change happen. And, if you look closely at the work of the person you admire the most, you will realise that you are different from one another and that, actually, there is no one in the world who does exactly what you do the way that you do it.

You are one of a kind. This, by default, means that what you have to offer is original, precious, and infinitely valuable, because no one else is quite like you. No one else has your story. You are the only one who had your family and upbringing. No one sees the world the same way you do. No one has the same personality as you. Your quirks, characteristics, and strengths are a one-off, never-to-be-repeated blend. No one else has the same combination of skills and gifts as you.

Your unique talents have been shaped by the experiences you have had from the second you were conceived right up until this moment, tragedies and breakthroughs included - and the world needs those talents. Regardless of how successful and famous another person appears to be, there are still millions of people you can help, serve, touch, move, or inspire by blazing your trail. YOUR trail. Not someone else's. Yours.

We miss out on all manner of opportunities when we compare ourselves, our results, and our lives to people who we think have 'made it'. In fact, it could be said that nothing kills off creativity, innovation, and progress faster than obsessing about what the rest of the world is doing and what the people before you have already achieved.

Glossy pictures of attractive people, industry leaders, celebrities, and the world's rich and famous are plastered all over the internet and in print media, but what most people forget is that what is seen on the surface is rarely an accurate reflection of the truth.

In many cases, what we see looking in from the outside of someone else's life can be a different story altogether to what happens behind the scenes. If you could see the whole picture, you would surely begin to put more faith in your own journey instead of holding back from your dream thinking that you are inferior.

Not one single person on this planet is exempt from experiencing challenges, and even when you achieve fame and fortune, you will still have obstacles to overcome. It is simply unavoidable, for ourselves and our heroes alike. That is why believing that someone else has a so-called perfect life will only serve as a distraction to your career and what you can accomplish. You will lose precious energy and time that could have been invested into making your life as meaningful as it can be.

There is more to the story of those you look up to and the people you wish you were more like, and reaching the top is rarely a smooth ride. Often it is the complete opposite, as big results don't just happen on their own - they take work. So, when you see or meet a person who has achieved something extraordinary - whether winning an award, becoming wildly successful, or running a multi-million dollar company - start asking questions instead of shrinking into the shadows.

What struggles did they face to build their career? What adversity drove them to become the best in their field? How did they earn what they have today? What price did they pay to be who and where they are? What difficulties are they facing, or have they faced, that perhaps people don't know about?

By doing so, you will feel a deep sense of respect for the work the person has done; tens of thousands of sit-ups to be the highest-paid fighter, two thousand keynote speeches to be a top presenter, millions of words in drafts and discarded ideas in rubbish bins to write a book that reaches readers across the planet.

You will see their endless devotion to their vision, their purpose, and their goal, even in the moments when it seemed pointless or hopeless. You will realise that great achievement rarely happens without an enormous investment - and often, by putting everything on the line - and that struggle often precedes success. And if you look close enough at their history, careers, and lives, you will probably realise that when it comes down to it, you wouldn't trade places with them. If you did, you wouldn't get to be you, which truly is the privilege of a lifetime.

The surface appearance of anyone's life rarely provides a full picture, and so to judge someone's results, wealth, or lifestyle from a few interactions alone is like judging nature based on one season. A person who looks like they've had a smooth journey to the top may often have struggled the most to get there. Likewise, a person who looks like they will never make it can be two days away from the breakthrough that changes their life forever.

I've met influencers with a huge following who feel lonely and spent time with people who look like they have it all but who have no idea what their purpose is. By looking beyond the surface, you will discover a deeper truth: that there is not only room for you in the world but that the most important thing you can do is to allow yourself to rise to the top.

No matter who we are, we have something that someone else wants or needs - a gift worth sharing - but if we are too busy focusing on other people's lives, we may never connect with it in ourselves. This is why if you keep checking the social media profiles and tracking the careers of the people you think have more and do more than you, you will miss out on the invaluable opportunities that are around you right now. The result of this is that your career will grow at a snail's pace.

So, consider this: what would happen if you showed up every day, whether you win, lose, or draw, instead of hiding in the shadows of other people? What if you invested as much time into your own goals as you do in reading about what other people have done? How would you start to feel about yourself? What would happen in your career if you watered your own grass instead of continually peeking over the fence at someone else's backyard?

The achievements of the people you respect and admire might serve as inspiration to show you what is possible. But let that be all that it is - inspiration - and then return to building the career you aspire to have today so you can experience it tomorrow.

You are needed. The difference you want to make, that you are capable of making, hasn't been made yet. You were born for it. That leader, speaker, or author hasn't said it the way you will. That musician hasn't poured their heart into every note of their songs the way you will. That painter hasn't created work that is dripping with the very essence of their soul the way you will. That teacher hasn't taught what you will teach. That entrepreneur hasn't solved the problem you will. That scientist hasn't made the breakthrough you will, and that healer hasn't healed the people you will. They don't have your spirit.

So, be the missing piece. Look at the world around you and care greatly about what you see as well as what you can do to make an impact. Focus on who you are here for, not on the accomplishments of other individuals or how small you think your achievements are in comparison. Focus on the lives you have already touched and will touch and not on the little voices inside your head that tell you that you aren't capable of great things.

And, above all, focus on what you can do today that will make a difference in your life and in the lives of so many others tomorrow, and not on what happened yesterday or who is making history right now. Keep in mind that most people aren't even trying to impact the world and that those who are have had their fair share of struggles, too. So, don't let the illusion of success distract you from what you are here to do because there is room for you at the top.

Get Ready for the Spotlight

Close your eyes. Breathe in. Look inside your heart. What do you see yourself doing in the world? What all-important work are you focused on? Where are you travelling to? What are you saying? Who are you being? How many people are you influencing? And what difference are you making in their lives?

Deep within you, you know what significant work you want to do. You know who you most want to move, touch, and inspire through the music you write, the companies you build, the art you create, or the healing you facilitate. You know how many lives you want to impact in your career.

The next question is: are you ready for it? If one million people saw your creations, read your writings, or heard you speak tomorrow, would you be prepared for everything that might follow? If you were interviewed about your life and accomplishments on national television next week, would you feel ready?

If you received the opportunity to speak in front of the United Nations, pitch your business idea to a room full of investors, or present to the CEO of a Fortune 500 company this month, would you know what to say? If you received 250,000 hits on your website this year, would you have something to offer those eager eyes? Are you ready for the spotlight and for those who need you?

The world is overflowing with people who have the potential to touch humanity in a meaningful way and who, if given the chance, could impact the lives of millions with their work. Despite this, so few people are prepared for the impact and success that they aspire to and dream of, which prevents them from going to the next level.

However, we can prepare ourselves for the career we dream of much the same way a high-level athlete would prepare for the Olympics. So, start preparing yourself for the spotlight by deciding what the ultimate accomplishment in your career would be. What would you love to do and experience in your career? What would being the best in your field look like? Are you doing today what will lead to the results you desire tomorrow?

It is far more difficult to pack for a trip when you have no idea where you are going. This is why knowing what the career of your dreams looks like is the first step in taking yourself there as, once you know what you are aiming to achieve, you can start training yourself for it. You can get to work on moving forwards to where you want to be.

One day while writing *Born Great*, I was working in a health food café where I met a 19-year-old man named Tristan. During our conversation, he asked me what I was writing about. After responding that the book is about pursuing your purpose in life, I found out that his dream was to become a professional basketball player. Here's what his schedule looked like on an average day: sleep, train at the gym, go to work, play basketball, and sleep. Little else mattered to him outside of his pursuit to play and master the sport. He was diligently training himself for his dream.

While we each have a gift that we can build our careers and lives around, it rarely comes out of the box ready to go. We need to work to perfect it, polish it, and turn it into something that is ready for the world. This often means millions of written words for a writer to find their flow, thousands of hours of training to become a winning athlete, and several failed attempts before making a breakthrough in a business that goes global. But, this is how we get to where we want to be; we practise so much that we reach a stage where people can't help but notice who we are. When your dream career matters greatly to you, you will apply yourself to reach that level.

There is no doubt that growing this career will require humility, dedication, and devotion. There will be times where you must sacrifice lesser pursuits to channel your focus and energy into the task at hand. Those sacrifices, both great and small, will help you reach where you would love to be. This is especially relevant for the most inspiring and important goals of your career.

These sacrifices might include putting relationships on hold, limiting your social life temporarily, and eating an exemplary diet so that you can move upward and forward. Making these sacrifices will allow your greatest pursuit to become your only pursuit. Eventually, you will reach a tipping point where all your hard work pays off and you find yourself reaching levels greater than ever before. When this happens, you won't regret the sacrifices you made to get there. You will only regret not having devoted yourself to your purpose sooner.

What you achieve in your career rests as much on your relationship with yourself as it does on the work you do to get there. If you are going to be known to people across the globe, then you need to know yourself intimately. That is, you need to know who you are, what you stand for, what you stand against, and what your life's mission is.

You will need to figure out why being known matters; perhaps because you have a mission to fulfil or an example to set. You will need to be crystal clear on the message you want to share as well as who that message is for. Then, you need to be willing to stand by those: to be who you are, speak your truth, and share your message.

To do this, you need to embrace yourself wholeheartedly and back yourself endlessly. Do you believe to your core that you have been perfectly designed to fulfil your destiny? That there is an important role carved out just for you in this world? If you feel in any way ashamed of who you are, then you are casting shadows over yourself. But embracing who you are for all that you are and all that you are not - that is the key to a thriving career and a life that flourishes.

So often, we try to show off what we think is our best side, hoping that people won't see our weaknesses. We attempt to do what we think others want us to do and say what we think they want to hear, which limits what we can do, experience, and achieve.

We reject ourselves on the inside, so then it feels natural when we aren't chosen for the gig we want or the biggest opportunities. Yes, we may secretly feel sad about missed chances and all that didn't come our way, but how can you be seen and appreciated by a million people if you aren't willing to see and appreciate yourself first? If you are hiding, then they can't see you and I can't see you, and if we can't see you, then we can't know you nor experience your gift.

Being in the spotlight will require you to take down the walls between yourself and the people around you. The more you heal your relationship with yourself, the more your life and work will expand. As this happens, you will see how your unique abilities - those you might have previously thought were strange or peculiar - are actually your competitive advantage, and how this personal edge of yours is the reason you will make an impact, not the reason you don't deserve to.

The need to seek validation for yourself, your beauty, your skills, and your work will fade away. You will no longer spend your time trying to prove your worth to people, and in relinquishing this, you will be free to express yourself from the heart. You will allow your life to be guided by your soul, your vision, and your destiny - your true north.

Essentially, you will be far better equipped to share what is within you with millions of people if you do it from a strong foundation of unconditional love. Why? Because if you know exactly who you are and what you are here for, you will be able to withstand any outside opinion or people who try to knock you off your path.

Are you willing to do this? To accept yourself no matter what? To leave your imprint in the lives of hundreds or thousands or millions of people, you need to be all of who you are, not just small pieces of who you are. If you keep trying to hide your true self, afraid that people won't understand you, then the world won't experience the magic and beauty that is already within you.

With every part of you that you choose to embrace with your whole heart, you will awaken new potential and, with that potential, will come new opportunities. You will reach into the lives of more people who need and want what you have to offer and experience the heart-opening moments that occur when you change the world by being exactly who you are.

No one holds you back more than you hold yourself back. After all, it is you who decides that you are ready for the spotlight. You decide that you can be an inspiration to others, that your story is worth hearing, that your work is worth experiencing, and that you are worth knowing. You don't have to wait for someone else to give you permission to build the career you dream of; you can start now. You can choose to stand out by being who you are - your authentic self.

So, love yourself in the places where you are tender, so that any self-doubt from yesterday no longer defines what you can achieve tomorrow. Be willing to work on yourself and your craft until you know to your core that you are ready to be seen for all that you are and all that you do. Finally, do everything you can today to prepare yourself for the career you dream of because you are the stained-glass window through which your soul shines its light into the world.

Make Your Mark on the World

As you pursue your purpose and grow the career of your dreams, you are bound to encounter criticism. Something you do or say will get on the wrong side of someone and they will challenge you because of it. Someone will disagree with your perspective, try to compete against you, attempt to take you down, or dislike your work, speech, music, or ideas.

You might enter into disagreements with people, encounter dissatisfied customers or unhappy fans, have your motives questioned, or even be attacked publicly. At other times, you will need to intentionally stir up the status quo in order to make your difference, from ending relationships to challenging the popular opinion.

Unfortunately, most people are terrified of having their character and work criticised, of falling short in their results, of their boss critiquing their creation, or of failing an audition. As a result, they don't dare share their next idea, try their hand at something new, or launch themselves forwards in the direction they want to go.

Instead of aiming for the bigger goal, they take the safe route instead; the one that has already been walked by people before them. They barely play the game let alone play to win. But the key to rising up and succeeding is not in avoiding criticism altogether. It is in not allowing the conflicts and criticisms you experience to deter you from the moves you need to make - the ones that will skyrocket your career into the stratosphere.

How do you know that you are holding back on your purpose because you are afraid of the criticism that might come your way? Well, you bite your tongue instead of speaking your mind. You put off finishing that creation or giving that talk for fear that people will rip it (and you) apart. You worry about what people will think of your plans, so you keep them quiet. You hide, trying to avoid any situation where you might put yourself forward and be judged.

But here is a truth worth embracing: the greater your courage to stand in the fire and burn, the greater your life can become. However, if you continue to let the fear of being criticised get the better of you, it may cost you your dreams as well as the opportunity to be seen, known, and heard by the world around you.

As you grow, people will judge the way you live and the choices you make. They will tell their friends if they like you and, if they don't, they will likely tell people why. To some, you will be the best thing since sliced bread while others might think you have a screw loose. For every person who agrees with what you do there will be someone who thinks you are missing the mark completely. Some people will think you are courageous for starting a business and others will think that you are crazy for giving up the security that often comes with a job.

You might also experience relationships where the person likes you at first but ends up resenting you, or the opposite, where they dislike you at first before respecting you enormously. You may have experienced this too, where sometimes you get along with someone like a house on fire and sometimes it's as cold as ice from the day you meet, even if you have no idea why.

Sometimes you feel infinitely inspired by one mentor but can't understand why people pay for advice from another. All of the above is not wrong or bad; it is just human dynamics at work. The problem exists if you become emotionally reliant on being liked, you will soon end up doubting yourself at every turn as you try to please everyone else but you.

I learned many years ago that my time is far better spent serving the people who appreciate my presence and need my gifts rather than trying to convert those who don't. I also learned that if I don't click with someone upon first meeting them, I sometimes just need to allow time for us to build rapport as it's not always 'love at first sight'.

But in the grand scheme of it all, I don't believe it is worth sacrificing your precious time and valuable energy begging and pleading to another human being just so they will say you are worthy, credible, beautiful, noble, generous, or morally sound (according to their personal views).

There are more than seven billion people alive today, so it doesn't make sense to let one tiny opinion hold you back from your dream. Sometimes there is nothing we can do to alter a person's perception of us, and if we run around trying to control how the outside world sees us, we will waste our life away. My advice? Don't alter what you do to please a small handful of people. Instead, focus on the next most important thing you can do to fulfil your purpose and keep the criticism you receive in perspective along the way.

If you go through life keeping a list of the people who criticised you and label them as toxic, you will end up living in a bubble, feeling disempowered, depressed, and disconnected. So, to make sure that you don't give up during critical times in your journey, learn to handle criticism if and when it comes your way.

Ask yourself useful questions like: what pushed a button for this person when they read, saw, or heard (x)? What do they feel and why? What is happening in their world? Then use these insights to decide on the best course of action, which could be to speak your truth or say nothing at all (this might take inner strength if you are fiery like me).

Pay attention to the source of the criticism. Is it coming from a customer? A friend? A fan? Or from someone you don't know and will never do business with? As a general rule, I don't recommend taking advice about your business, your work, or your life from people who are uninspired or on an entirely different path to you. And if you are ever criticised for your personal character, ask yourself this: "Would I trade lives with this person?" The answer is likely to liberate you every single time.

During my career, I have been told I have no compassion, that my love is empty, and that I have no ability to care about another individual. Harsh, I know, and all based on someone's limited perspective of who I am. In each situation, I saw how I had challenged the person by going against their rules or defying their assumption of who they thought I was. Although it sometimes felt that way, I knew that it was never about me - it was about them - and that nothing people say can reflect the whole truth about who I am.

The same principle applies to you. How could what they say be the truth, when they've only known you for a few days, weeks, or months, and you've known yourself your whole life? The opinion that matters the most is your own, and their opinion is based on their own experiences, not the core of who you are. As the multi-million dollar property tycoon, Grant Cardone, said, "Some people think I'm inspiring, some people think I'm arrogant. I guess it depends what you're looking for."

Don't allow the opinions of those who don't understand or appreciate you, or those who are uninspired and disempowered, to be a reason to give up on what you were born to do, and do not change who you are because someone can't handle you and what you do. It's impossible to throw a stone in the pond without making a ripple - and you were born to make waves in the world. So, next time you receive critical feedback about your character or the work you have done, remember these powerful words from Theodore Roosevelt:

"It is not the critic who counts; not the man who points out how the strong man stumbles, or where the doer of deeds could have done them better. The credit belongs to the man who is actually in the arena, whose face is marred by dust and sweat and blood; who strives valiantly; who errors, who comes short again and again, because there is no effort without error and shortcoming; but who does actually strive to do the deeds; who knows great enthusiasms, the great devotions; who spends himself in a worthy cause; who at the best knows in the end the triumph of high achievement, and who at the worst, if he fails, at least fails while daring greatly, so that his place shall never be with those cold and timid souls who neither know victory nor defeat."

I say: let the spectators yell and scream all they want because you are the one on the playing field. You are the one with a chance of winning the game. At the end of the day, you will be the one holding the trophy and being rewarded for your hard work in the pursuit of greatness, not them.

You will live with the deep satisfaction of knowing that you have applied yourself, invested in your dream, and grown as a result of it. And your spectators? They will be exactly where they are today ten years down the line, because they were too busy focusing on other people's shortcomings to face and work on their own lives and dreams.

So, hear the voices but don't allow them to drown out what your heart is telling you. Continue to connect with the highest counsel there is - your soul - and let it guide you every step of the way. Above all else, believe in your destiny, because you were made for it and it was made for you. Remember: outside opinion is merely commentary to the game you are playing.

*****

You are extraordinary. You have wisdom to teach, skills to share, and solutions to give, and you do have it in you to serve thousands of people if you feel called to. So, remember that you are not alone on the journey of growing a career that inspires and ignites you, and the more love you pour into your career, the further you will go.

Keep in mind that strategies, customers, and growth ideas will come and go, but the reason you started in the first place will be your greatest source of inspiration as the journey unfolds. Finally, step forward each day ready to serve, and use your career as a way to share your heart with the world. You can do this, and you deserve to grow the career of your dreams.

11

You Can Fly to Great Heights

*"Reach high, for stars lie hidden in your soul.
Dream deep, for every dream precedes the goal."*

Pamela Vaull Starr

Your dream for the future is the destination you aspire for, and, with air beneath your wings, you can take off and fly to great heights. You can see inspiring places, meet incredible people, feel a deep sense of meaning every day, and experience things so beautiful they make your heart ache. But to fulfil your purpose in such a magnificent way, you must understand that in order to thrive on the journey ahead, you must take care of your greatest asset: YOU.

Are you committed to nourishing yourself every day so that you can rise up, time and time again? Are you devoted to supporting yourself so that the road doesn't wear you down? Are you willing to trust yourself wholeheartedly, every step of the way?

If you are, you will quickly find yourself moving from strength to strength. Ideas and inspiration will flow to you with ease, solutions will fall into your lap, and doors will open for you wherever you go.

Energy, focus, and discipline will be abundant and, sooner than you can imagine, you will have carved out the life and career you've been waiting for.

Connect With Your Heart and Soul

Life is full of evolution. Billions of people are moving, growing, and striving simultaneously. The Earth keeps spinning, cities keep growing, millions of businesses keep selling and serving, and people keep living and dying. Because of this, we are bombarded with an endless stream of noise every day: opinions, advertising, current affairs, news, and media. All you need to do to experience it is walk down a main street, turn on a television, or log on to social media for five minutes.

It's no wonder that in this sea of endless noise, so many people feel distracted, empty, confused, and lost. When we become so tuned in to the world around us that we become disconnected from the world within us, we struggle to connect with who we truly are and lose touch with our sense of destiny. This costs us enormously in terms of our achievements and our ability to fulfil our purpose.

But, when we learn to tune out from the noise and turn inwardly to connect with our heart and soul, we find the answers to the greatest questions we will ever ask about who we are, the life we are born to live, and the next step of our journey. This is true for every single human being.

Your heart and soul are faultless navigation systems designed to guide, push, pull, nudge, and call you towards your destiny. They are present in every breath you take, from birth to death. They are the greatest allies you will ever have, and all they want for you is to do what you came to Earth to do: what you are capable of. The more deeply you connect with them, the further forward you can go and the further outward you can reach.

In the moments where you connect with your heart, you discover who you are, and not a distorted image of who you think you are, but your true, authentic self. In doing this, you appreciate your divine design, your God-given blueprint, your unique beauty, and your unrivalled originality. A quiet confidence will emerge from your core as you not only know who you are but feel privileged to be you.

When you connect with your soul, you befriend a GPS system that can help you navigate your way to an amazing life. You will receive guidance through intuitive nudges or direct messages that tell you where to go and what to do. You will discover what your 'thing' is, your sweet spot in the universe. You will feel enlivened by the conscious connection with your destiny every day. The more frequently you commune with both your heart and soul, the clearer you will be about the life you want to create for yourself and the actions you need to take to create it.

One of the most powerful ways to connect with your heart and soul is to develop a spiritual practice. This practice needs to suit you and help you to connect with the sanctuary within yourself - a sanctuary that you can visit every day. It will provide you with the time and space to process your thoughts and feelings, receive creative ideas, and listen to your heart and soul daily, which are all foundations for a long and lasting career and extraordinary life. Beyond this, it will nourish you in ways that food, sleep, and your relationships will not.

The first time I consciously chose to engage in a spiritual practice was at the young age of 17. I used writing, self-development books, and affirmations to care for myself emotionally and strengthen my spiritual connection. While studying at university the following year, I kept a diary to continue deepening and expanding my awareness. Every day, I would use a blank page to interpret my dreams, messages I'd received from the world around me, significant things people had said to me that day, and other relevant thoughts and feelings. I participated in and accelerated my personal growth this way for 12 months.

Through my twenties, this spiritual practice evolved into an extensive application of the self-growth tools I had learned, and finally, into a journaling practice that is a blend of all of the above. As my career continued to grow, I began journaling approximately 10,000 words a month.

Using my journal as a free space to explore the depths of my heart and mind, I documented significant moments and realisations. This practice supported me to heal after relationship break-ups, find peace of mind in trying times, remain focused in my career, access guidance and direction for the future, and receive countless ideas for pieces of inspired writing.

It continues to help me in this way today, and I wouldn't be who or where I am had this practice not become an intrinsic part of my life at such a young age. In fact, I may not have made it through depression as a teenager had I not set a strong personal foundation in place before I hit rock bottom.

This practice, together with the work I have done to develop my career, has helped me to experience what I can only describe as a magnificent unfolding of my purpose on Earth. Your spiritual practice can be the same for you; one of the most powerful companions you have as you scale the mountain.

Since it comes naturally to me, it's no surprise that I use writing to access my heart and soul. But there are many ways to engage in a spiritual practice that unites you with your inner, higher self. You might find it in yoga classes that strengthen your body and enhance your connection to your dharma. You might find it through long walks in nature where you connect with the spirit and beauty of the Earth. You might find it while watching the night sky, listening to inspiring music, or travelling the world.

Each expression is equally powerful, and what matters is not how you connect with your heart and soul, but that you do. It matters that you make time to quieten your mind and go within so that you can discover the many treasures that await you. After all, how can you grow an inspiring business if you aren't connected to your deepest driving force? How can you feel the love you yearn for in your relationships if you aren't connected to the love that lives inside your own heart? And how can you create a future that fulfils you if you have no idea what matters to you?

Retreating from the outside world will aid you in connecting with your inner self not only today, but on every step of your journey from this moment forward. At many times in the future, you will look for answers about what move to make next, which direction to go in, what course to study, which mentor to take on, or how to solve a problem you face. As you encounter these defining moments, you will be required to slow down in order to speed up and seek insight from within.

You have no idea just how much wisdom awaits you once you tune in to your inner self. Each and every time that you become quiet and source counsel from within you, you will be rewarded with clarity. It is the source of everything you seek: the spark of the life you want, the career you desire the most, the success and achievement you feel you are capable of, and the sense of purpose that you crave.

So, when will you unplug - from technology, from what people think, and from the busyness of everyday life - and retreat to the sanctuary of stillness inside you? When will you realise that there is no counsel wiser than that which flows from the core of your being? And when will you stop looking for the next step from the voices around you instead of looking within for the roadmap to your future? Deep within you, you have inspiring answers to questions about where you are going, why your life has unfolded the way it has, and why you are here at all. You just need to take the time to reflect inwardly to discover them.

The world is full of people all going in different directions and connecting with your heart and soul will help you find yours. That is the race that really matters. No voice counts more than the voice that is within you, no love is more important for you to feel than your own, and no wisdom or insight from the outside is superior to your own when it comes to your future. When you connect with your heart and soul, you have access to all of this and so much more, including the keys to the life you can't wait to live.

A life enriched by connecting with your heart is one worth living for, and a life guided by your soul is one worth experiencing. So, don't spend your life so caught up in other people's lives that you miss out on your own. Instead, allow the endless stream of noise from the world around you to become a distant whisper so you can hear all that is within you and guiding you to live the way you dream. Remove yourself from conversations that waste time, environments that drain you, and social idealisms that don't inspire you. Follow your true north. It knows the way.

Replace the trivial with the meaningful. Look within you as much as you look around you. Go inward so you can move forward. Learn to find stillness in your daily life. Allow yourself to be guided and awakened by the power of the love and spirit within you. Connect with your heart and soul every single day. For then, and only then, will you know exactly what to do next to fulfil the undeniable calling for which you were born - your destiny.

Master Your Patience and Persistence

Anything worth achieving, from raising a child to writing a book or growing a global brand, will require patience and persistence in equal measures. When applied at the right time, your inner patience and persistence will make sure that you don't give up right before you succeed spectacularly in your career and life. They will make sure that you continue to pursue your dream, no matter what roadblock you come across, and enable you to reap and enjoy the many fruits of your labour along the way.

Patience can be defined as our ability to remain level-headed when we experience delays, problems, or obstacles on the path to our goal. Often referred to as a virtue worth having, patience is our capacity to withstand the challenges we face while keeping a steadfast focus on the outcome in mind. Expressing patience might not come naturally to you, especially when you can see the places you can go and you want to be there right now. However, doing so is essential as patience allows the stillness that is required to make big breakthroughs.

Patience provides the space for you to think and feel things through. It gives you time to reflect inwardly and decide which actions, tasks, and projects matter the most so that each day of your life is lived on purpose. Patience teaches us that, just because we cannot see the end result today, it doesn't mean that it isn't manifesting or that we won't ever achieve it.

It reminds us that nature and life have cycles within them - they ebb and flow - which frees us from stressful ideas, such as thinking that we should be able to go from zero to millionaire overnight or from start-up to award-winning company inside a week. It teaches us that it is often when we are the most present, and thus patient, that we are the most powerful. It also reminds us that small actions add up over time and that it is what we do daily that builds our destiny. After all, success happens one step at a time and not all of those steps will be giant leaps.

What if the level you want to reach in your career takes twice as long as originally planned? Are you going to give up on your dream because of it? Or will you express the patience required - with yourself, people, and the way the world works - to see your plans through to fruition, regardless of whether that happens in two or ten years?

Here's an even more pertinent question: is what you are aspiring for so important and meaningful to you that you are willing to work and wait long enough to achieve it? This is the power of patience: it makes sure that we stick around long enough to see our success manifest right before our eyes.

Too often, we try to pull the plant out of the ground before it has had time to take root and break through the surface. We want the magic pill that doubles our income, expands our fame, and fixes our health overnight. This impatience causes us to abort plans before they've had a chance to produce results and give up on ourselves before giving our dreams a proper shot.

If you are too busy rushing from one destination to another, you might miss important clues, guidance, ideas, and details that will help you flourish in your career and wealth, not to mention miss out on the great adventure of life. In my opinion, walking away from your heartfelt dream because more time and energy is required to see it through to its manifestation is a heavy burden to carry.

Persistence relates to our willingness to continue moving towards a goal despite the difficulty it might involve. We draw on persistence when taking action and when we come across a rough patch of road. It is the 'get things done' energy that gives us the momentum we need to climb mountains and the strength and determination required to produce extraordinary results.

It is in those moments when you are keeled over crying and you feel like you haven't got anything left in your tank that persistence rises up from within you and says, "I've got this," and, "Let's do this." Persistence says "Yes" to conquering obstacles so that you can achieve what you care about the most.

Even if you do experience breakdowns along the way where it feels like your whole world has collapsed, you will fight back. No matter how many times you fall down, you will find a way to get back on your feet again. You will not let failure, or a broken dream, extinguish your spirit. Instead, you will use everything you encounter to help you in any and every way that you can.

Each time you experience a defeat, persistence will get you through. It is the outward expression of courage. It is inner strength in motion. It is where true human greatness can be witnessed. It is when you will do whatever it takes to stay on the path you know is your own.

Both patience and persistence refer to our willingness to stand strong and remain centred in the face of discomfort and obstacles. They come from the same place within us, except one is passive and the other is active. Patience 'is' and persistence 'does'.

With patience, you wait, knowing that this too shall pass, and that life has a plan for the situation you find yourself in. With persistence, you grit your teeth and keep going, knowing that your hard work will pay off, even if it hurts right now. Wisdom is knowing how, when, and where to apply each one to help you move forward towards your goals.

Let's say that you want to increase your muscle tone and physical strength. There is no doubt that transforming your body will require patience and persistence in great degrees, through challenging workouts, hiring a personal trainer, changing your diet, and experiencing delayed onset muscle soreness. Persistence will get you into the gym on cold and early mornings, help you to push through your pain barrier to complete your workouts, and achieve new personal bests.

If you have trained for any length of time, you know that not every session will be your best one. Sometimes you will bound into the gym with determination, and other times you will feel so tired that it will seem like you've gone backwards. One week, you will think you're a hulk and the next week you will feel weak and unfit. But with persistence in the right measure, you will show up for yourself regardless of how you feel that day. Why? Because you know you won't regret overcoming temporary discomfort to achieve your result and every effort counts.

You also know that you won't form a six-pack in three training sessions any more than you will drop ten kilograms in two weeks. This is where patience will be your ally in achieving your goal. Without it, you will have a go-hard-or-go-home training style, where you work out intensely for a few weeks and then give up before you have had a chance to see results. Patience will remind you that achieving the outcome you want involves as much rest and recovery outside the gym as it does effort and dedication inside the gym and that your body will also require adequate protein, water, nutrition, and deep sleep to undergo a metamorphosis.

You need both patience and persistence to succeed, and the same principle applies for growing a career centred around your purpose, regardless of whether that is finding your dream job or building a business. There will be times when you need to move forward boldly to get to where you want to be and times where you simply need to wait.

There will be times where it's on you to get things done and times when you need to allow your actions to generate results. Sometimes making progress involves taking a giant leap, which requires all the persistence you can muster. Other times, it's all about the small actions that add up over time, where patience is needed to do what will make the difference in the long run.

If you apply too much patience to your dream, you will leave your future to chance, believing that it will all happen if and when it is 'meant to'. This will cost you the results that come from taking equal amounts of action to create the life that you want. On the other hand, if you apply too much persistence, you may run yourself into the ground and experience burnout.

But if you listen to your heart each day, your intuition will guide you on which one to draw on, when, and to what degree. Ask yourself, "Does it serve my goal to be patient or persistent right now?" and, "Is this better off in my hands or in the hands of life in this moment?"

The willpower that persistence offers and the wisdom that patience brings will help you to do the big and small things necessary to succeed and make your impact on the planet. So, be patient when it is time to let the plant grow and persistent when you need to get in gear and move forward. Balance letting it happen with making it happen, so you can build momentum towards your dreams and experience the life that is possible for you.

Look After Your Home on Earth

Your physical body is your only point of contact with planet Earth. Without it, you aren't here. It gives your soul a home in the world, and its purpose is to help you fulfil your purpose. It carries every single thing that you feel and everything that you think, and it makes possible every single thing that you say, do, create, and experience while you are alive. It is because of your hands that you can hold this book, because of your eyes that you can read it, because of your brain that you can comprehend it, and because of your heart that you can feel it.

Your body makes you possible. It makes it possible for people to know, learn from, and be inspired by you. No matter what your dream is, your body enables you to fulfil it, and no matter what your inspiration, your body makes it possible for you to follow it. It is the instrument through which your soul plays its song in the world.

Your body enables you to experience the precious gift of being alive. If you don't care for it, that gift diminishes and, eventually, vanishes. But if you honour your body, then you will thrive every day of your life.

Think about your relationship with your body. Do you nourish it or ignore what it needs? Do you understand how it works? Do you appreciate it or wish it was different? Taller, smaller, thinner, stronger? Do you honour its natural cycles and alternating rhythms, or do you drown out your life force with caffeine and chemicals?

The unfortunate truth is that most people treat their body poorly, like it's a dumping ground for an unfulfilling life. They write off their symptoms, skip the treatment they need, and disregard what their body is saying to them. In doing so, they destroy one of the greatest teammates they will ever have.

I awakened to the power, beauty, and importance of my body after experiencing physical burnout in my late twenties. After founding my company, I ran myself into the ground. For the first year, I showed up for everyone else before myself. I took on too many roles and responsibilities, burning the candle at both ends.

Instead of deciding how I would run the day, the day ran me. I felt overwhelmed and it began to show physically. I put on weight, ate comfort foods late at night, and felt frazzled. I reached a point where I could see where I wanted to go with my career, but it felt like my car wouldn't start to take me there. I felt defeated. It was saddening and frustrating.

One afternoon, I was resting on my bed with my hands on my abdomen thinking about my life and work. Suddenly, I pictured my organs underneath the surface of my skin, each fulfilling their own role to keep me alive and functioning. That's when it hit me: my body wasn't made of metal and yet I had been treating it like a machine, pushing it to the limit and expecting it to perform seven days a week without proper care and maintenance.

Confronted by my mortality and how sensitive my physiology was, I decided to take my health seriously. I knew, then and there, that if I didn't start valuing my well-being and begin looking after my body, the books I wanted to write and the difference I wanted to make wouldn't and couldn't happen. That was the day my journey into the study of neuroscience, nutrition, clean eating, and the healing world of Ayurvedic medicine began. From then onward, my knowledge of my body and its essential functions grew, as did my desire to take care of my home on Earth.

My greatest lesson on this journey was that supporting your body to support you happens one decision at a time. And so, how you feel physically today is, in large part, a result of the decisions you made yesterday and in the many days before that. The food you have eaten, the products you have used, the movements you have made, and the fluids you have consumed have brought you to where you are now and have either helped or hindered you.

Ayurvedic medicine teaches that each piece of food you consume takes 36 days to assimilate into all seven layers of tissue in your body. This means that the food you eat on day one of a food plan will literally become part of your blood, tissues, bones and other parts of your body over the next month. It is the principle of compounding applied to your physical body, and the result you experience depends on what you do, moment by moment and day by day.

The way I see it is this: why would you allow sugary treats to undermine the progress you want to make in your career? Or why would you eat foods that slow and weigh you down, making it harder to think clearly and excel at your purpose? Why wouldn't you want to prolong your life so that you can experience more of what you love?

It's easy to say that one poor food choice doesn't matter, but it does. Why? Because it is those moments where you say, "Oh, I'll just have one," and, "I'll burn it off at the gym later," that add up over time, until one day you wonder why you aren't bouncing out of bed in the morning or why you feel lethargic in the middle of the day.

Great achievement requires physical nourishment and you need it to see your future clearly and move towards it, no matter how inspired you are by what you do. So, focus on creating energy and radiance in your body, because if you don't have your own back, it will become difficult to support yourself when it counts the most.

Creating lasting wellness is as much a matter of mind over body as it is body over mind. So, start to listen more closely to what your body is saying to you. What changes is your body trying to guide you to make? Changes to the way you work? The way you eat? The way you spend your time? Where you are living? Who you are dating? The company you keep?

Your body knows you intimately, and so the moment you stop being true to yourself in any area of your life, it begins to break down. On the flipside, the moment you align with and do what is right for you, your wellness returns. Think about it: don't you have a far better chance of feeling vital if you wake up each day looking forward to what lies ahead instead of waking up dreading the next 24 hours? Don't you feel the most well on days where you do what you love as opposed to days where you drag your feet to work?

Your body is highly intelligent and innately connected to your soul - the core of who you are. It is tuned in like a GPS. No matter what is happening in your body presently, it is trying to tell you what you need to know and show you where you need to go. It is not random when you start feeling tired, off-colour, or flat when you are doing something that doesn't inspire you. Your body is attempting to tell you that the path you are on isn't the one for you (taking a high number of sick days from your job is a dead giveaway).

It is trying to help you master your destiny. Perhaps your body is prompting you, as mine did for me, to strip your life back to what matters the most and let the rest go. Or, maybe it is saying that it is time to take the leap of faith you've wanted to for so long. Regardless of the message, your body is crying out for you to listen to the wisdom inside you, and once you make the changes it wants you to make, it can heal.

Put simply, when you lighten the load you are carrying mentally, emotionally, and spiritually, your body no longer has to carry it for you, and it can begin to supply you with the fuel you need to get to your destination instead. This doesn't mean that you won't ever feel tired or unwell as you fulfil your purpose. It just means that you will understand the language your body speaks and see the symptoms you experience in a new light.

For example, there is a difference between feeling anxious because you are about to go on stage in front of 500 people and feeling anxious because you have to get up and go to a job you dislike. There is also a difference between feeling exhausted because you worked on your goals for eight hours straight and feeling tired because you are bored by what you are doing.

It mirrors your mind and feelings every single day. It becomes more alive as you get closer to the expression of your true self in the world. Your body wants to move and express itself in a dance with your purpose and it wants to function optimally so that it can help you do precisely what you were born to do. Your body loves you and is here to serve you. Are you serving it?

Even though it may not always seem that way, your body is on your side. It doesn't attack you unless you are attacking yourself, and it doesn't break down unless you are breaking down. It is wired to survive and thrive, and you can work with it to achieve that outcome or you can fight against it, which essentially translates into you fighting against yourself. The bottom line is that the more in tune you become with your physical system, the more it can guide you to fulfil your dreams.

To experience your full spirit and zest for life, commit to honouring your physical needs for nutrition, treatment, sleep, and movement. If you don't know what your needs are, take the time to find out. Why? Because everything you give to your body, it will give back to you ten-fold.

Perhaps you need different food to achieve wellness, or maybe what you really need is more spiritual nourishment and unconditional love. Maybe you need more sleep to function at your optimum, or maybe you just need to do what you love daily to tap into your vitality. Maybe you need a specialist to help you heal your body, or maybe what you really need is to heal the emotional pain from your past so you can start thriving. Regardless, choose what is life-sustaining, not life-draining. Find what nourishes you from the inside-out, from the top of your head to the tips of your toes. Respect it, appreciate it, and, above all, love it.

The simple truth is that you're no use to yourself or the world if your body is struggling. Remember that you need it in order to fulfil your purpose here. It is your vehicle to live, breathe, share in relationships, and experience life on Earth - and it is all yours, for an entire lifetime. What a miracle it is - truly.

So, give to your body so it can take you where you want to go. Treat it with respect, remembering that it is flesh and bones and that it needs to be cared for. When you're sleeping, rest deeply and prepare for the next day of your life. When you're awake, live on purpose.

Feel deep and endless gratitude every day for each organ, muscle, and feature of your incredible physical system. Support it to support you so that you can work together as a team and make sure that at the end of your time here on Earth, you have done all you wanted to do, said all that you wanted to say, and expressed all that was deep inside your heart.

*****

Flying to great heights in your career and life is a journey and, like with any journey you take, it will have twists and turns as you move from destination to destination. That is what transforms what would be an ordinary journey into the adventure of a lifetime. The secret to keep progressing towards your dream, no matter what crosses your path tomorrow, is to make sure that you have what you need to move forward every day.

It is to pay attention to the signposts along the way and listen to the counsel that comes from within you. It is to pick yourself up again, no matter how hard you may have fallen. It is to remember that, no matter how rough the terrain is today, life wants us to prosper, and that as long as you allow yourself to be supported, you can fulfil the inspiring destiny for which you were born.

12

The World Is Waiting for Your Greatness

> *"The true meaning of life is to plant trees under whose shade you do not expect to sit."*
>
> **Nelson Henderson**

So often, we are consumed by our fear of what might happen if we give our dream our all. We hold back, worrying about all that could go wrong if we let go of the shore and seek broader horizons. We worry that we won't make it financially if we start that business, that people won't like who we are or what we do, or that we will fall short in pursuit of what matters the most to us.

Maybe we won't make it big, achieve what we dream, sustain a relationship while we establish our career, or be able to break through the obstacles that stand in the way of us fulfilling our calling. It's easy to listen to these fears. After all, they are trying to keep us safe and prevent us from experiencing the pain that falls and failures often bring.

But I have to ask you this: what is it that truly matters in the end? When you reach the final days of your life and look back over all the years that have passed, what will you see? Will you see a life lived half in and half out or one where you held nothing back, even when it required courage from the deepest part of you?

It is often in times when we are faced with our own mortality that we realise how much our purpose matters and decide to take a risk on our dreams. But it is in learning to summon that courage every single day, no matter how ordinary the day may seem, that we can make our life matter - to ourselves and the world around us - and unleash the greatness inside us.

Grow Into Your Success

A raw disclaimer from me to you: expressing your greatness in the world won't be the easiest journey you take. In fact, it may be one of the most difficult things you do as you seek to be all that you are and do all that you can. Do we want the journey of fulfilling our purpose to be easy? Of course. Do we want to be able to click our fingers and be 'there' now without experiencing growing pains along the way? Yes.

But the reality is that creating the life and career you dream of will require more personal growth than anything else you have ever done. It will push you to limits you didn't know you had, invite you to continually change and expand the way you see yourself, and challenge you to love yourself more deeply than ever before.

It's not easy to write a book. It will cause you to question yourself, your message, and your work as you write. Page by page, it will refine and reveal who you are. It's not easy to build a business. It will break you open at times and make you wonder why you do what you do. It will teach you to ask for help, learn new skills, and go beyond anything that previously felt comfortable in the pursuit of a thriving career. You will have to step up to the plate and bat every day, no matter what the outcome is.

It's not easy to master your art form, stand up for what you believe in, or share your message on a global stage. You'll have to face and feel your emotions at times. You'll be asked to bear your soul and embrace who you were born to be. As a friend of mine once said to me, all of the above takes rare tenacity - the courage to follow what our heart guides us to do with abandon. Not only this, it requires us to evolve exponentially as we rise up to meet our destiny.

We rarely want to wait for our ship to come into the harbour. Instead, we want to be outrageously famous tomorrow or experience our success overnight. But what we don't realise, or perhaps don't appreciate enough, is that we need to grow into the triumph we yearn for. Put simply, you need to become the person who produces that famous work, who speaks with conviction, and who holds their own even when adversity strikes.

That's when greatness happens, and everything you meet on your path is training for the bigger game that you were born to play. And I mean, everything. It's all part of the plan to help you add value to the world and succeed beyond your wildest imagination. Each moment you have faced from your birth until today is precisely what you needed to shape you into the person you are capable of being. That means the heartbreak deepened your art, the pain improved your performance, the bankruptcy made you a world-class entrepreneur, and the endless existential search turned you into a guide for those who are lost.

I have never met a person who has achieved greatness who hasn't taken major risks, been tried and tested, or faced difficult situations along the way. On the contrary, they have put themselves on the line and been challenged time and time again for the vision they see and the dream they have - and they keep on doing it because it's what is required to go to the next level.

So, you are not 'there' yet. It's no reason to slink away with your tail between your legs. It's not the end of the world. In fact, it's just the beginning. Nobody - and I mean, nobody - starts out as a legend. Although some people have a natural talent for what they do (some might say they are gifted), every master had to complete their apprenticeship somewhere along the line.

Every dancer falls a thousand times before they deliver their winning performance. Every singer botches up the lyrics or forgets their cue hundreds of times before they sing flawlessly. Every financier makes poor investments on the path to create wealth. Every business owner encounters growing pains before they hit the big time. And every famous writer grapples with their consciousness, and even their conscience, before their words become known to the world.

This, right here, is what differentiates the champions from the rest; the wisdom that there is a journey the hero must undertake to succeed. It is the same for you too. The hurdles you face today are required for you to reach new peaks.

It's human nature to try and run from anything that challenges us, but the truth is that we need these challenges to accomplish great things. We try to avoid situations where we may experience failure, humiliation, or rejection, but the truth is that we grow exponentially in times when the heat is on and we feel the most vulnerable.

We rarely experience breakthrough moments in our career and income when everything is going smoothly. On the contrary, it is often when we are pushed beyond what we think we can do that our brilliance emerges. That is when we get out of the way and let magic happen, and the reason why setbacks are a rich source of growth and learning.

Yes, this path you are on today or the path you are about to embark upon will require courage. It will put you through the proverbial fire more times than you can imagine. But it's worth every heartache, every learning curve, every slip, and every fall. Why? Because this is the place that dreams come true and visions come to life, and you may never discover the infinite and extraordinary nature of who you are if you play it safe instead of surrendering to where your soul wants you to go.

As a writer, there is no greater satisfaction than knowing that what you have written has reached into the heart of another human being and supported them in some way. The more lives your words touch, the more fulfilling your own existence becomes and the more deeply you feel that your purpose is complete.

That desire to connect with humanity in this way has been with me since I realised at age 14 that I didn't just love to write, I was born to write. It is as strong at this moment as it was then, and no amount of personal adversity has extinguished that fire. In fact, each time I have encountered a challenge - from financial struggle to heartache in intimate relationships - my desire to be there in someone's hour of need through my words has only deepened. I doubt it will ever leave me until the day I draw my final breath.

Along the way, there have been times where I felt like I'd failed, that my books weren't enough, and where I thought my writing was total crap. On the flipside, there have been countless moments where tears ran down my face after hearing how significant my words had been for someone, like the moment when a woman wrote to tell me that my blog had inspired her to keep going during a time when she felt suicidal.

Moments like these are when you know that you are changing the world with your work. Each time they happen, you will be fuelled with the confidence to keep going; to continue upwards, forwards, and onwards. It is the greatest payment you can receive, and it happens not by hiding in the shadows but by being willing to go all in and allow the journey to shape and change you into who you were born to be.

If I did not grow and change as a woman, my writing would never evolve. If my heart never broke open or I never cried while putting a book together, I would not know the depths of a life spent following my calling, nor be able to bare my heart, mind, and soul on the page.

In exactly this way, the personal growth that you will experience as you pursue your purpose is the very thing that enables you to make the difference your heart yearns to make. Yes, sometimes that growth is difficult, but it is precisely what prepares you for new opportunities to develop your career and expand your impact on the planet.

Trust that no matter what happens, you can pick yourself up out of the dust and push forwards until you reach a breakthrough. So, when the road gets rough, focus on the qualities that your challenges are developing in you as a person. Are they developing wisdom in you? Are they teaching you how to connect with people heart-to-heart? Are they awakening your inner entrepreneur, leader, speaker, business guru, healer, or coach? Are they igniting courage within you? Are they helping you to expand your influence on the planet?

If you continue to do this, you will wake up one day, sooner than you think, living a life that is flooded with the accomplishments, experiences, people, and love you have been looking for all along. You will be surrounded by all the blessings that come as a result of growing into the success that is possible for you.

It's Your Time

Time is the most valuable resource we have. We don't own it, we don't know how much we have, and we don't know when it will run out.

It is a gift that has been given to us, and the length of time we have on Earth is an opportunity to find our gift and use it. Those who are careless with their time end up having it taken away, but those who cherish it are likely to live a long and fulfilling life full of inspiring moments and experiences.

Time is life. In other words, how you spend your time is how you spend your life, and what you do with your time determines the kind of life you live. Perhaps this hasn't occurred to you, but your time is ticking by as you sit there reading this. Every time your heart beats, a tiny piece of your future becomes your history. The question is, are you writing the story of your life? Or are you wasting this precious gift, one that is cut short for many, by letting trivial situations and drama run your days, weeks, months, years, and even decades?

It is often when people realise that they don't have all the time in the world - because of a near-death experience, turning 50, personal adversity, or a serious illness - that they get real and get on with what matters. But here's the thing: I don't want you to wait for a tragedy to happen before you start living fully. I don't want you to go through life thinking that everything else matters more than the dream inside your heart.

Instead, I want every second of every day to be flooded with great meaning. I want each moment of your time here to be consumed by the pursuits that mean the world to you. And I don't want you to waste another second suffering inside an empty existence. So, what are you waiting for? Take this moment and make it your own, in every way. If that means putting this book down and making progress on something that matters more, please do it.

Spend your life in environments that inspire you, as often as possible. Even if that means moving homes or flying to the other side of the world to find your mojo, make the effort to do it. At every opportunity, engage in conversations with people who are going places. Fill your social circles with big thinkers and big hearts. And above all, make it a habit to question every single task, invitation, appointment, and project before you let it become a part of your calendar and, therefore, your life. Ask yourself, "Does this truly matter?" and, "What will this add up to?" before devoting another second of your precious time towards it.

Instead of spending time, learn to invest time. View every second of the day as an opportunity to invest in the future you dream of and filter out anything that doesn't and won't count in the long run. Every time you say no to an uninspiring task or opportunity, you will be rewarded with fresh ideas, new inspiration, spiritual epiphanies, meaningful moments, or solutions you've been waiting for - and it will happen every single time, without fail.

When you waste your time, you waste who you are. In a nutshell, if you live a life filled with pointless activities or tasks that drain you, you are literally throwing away your potential. Most people don't grasp this intrinsic connection between their time and who they are, and so they never quite comprehend the true value of their presence.

As a result, they undercharge for their services, say yes to meetings they don't need to be at, take on responsibilities that weigh them down, and keep the kind of company that is less than stellar. To waste your time is to dilute the very essence of you. It dilutes what makes you so magnificent to begin with.

In the book titled *Deep Work,* university professor, Cal Newport, explored the power of focusing on a single intention for extended periods of time to accelerate progress towards 'wildly important goals'. As he wrote, "The ability to perform deep work is becoming increasingly rare at exactly the same time it is becoming increasingly valuable in our economy. As a consequence, the few who cultivate this skill, and then make it the core of their working life, will thrive."

In other words, the more time you devote to the work that will take both you and your career to the next level, the more masterful you will become and the faster you can scale to new achievements. You will create the momentum you want by doing the work that matters most. Your dedication will pay dividends as you will become so skilled, powerful, and influential that people will flock to you and send others your way.

The master recognises that mastery doesn't happen overnight. This wisdom, paired with their willingness to show up daily, is why they become masters. They humbly acknowledge that their next best work is always waiting for them around the corner, and they know that it is only through sitting with their work that they can see what must happen for that work to become profound, engaging, valuable, and inspiring.

Mastery doesn't happen without devotion and so, if you want to achieve mastery in your field, then treating your preparation time with reverence is the way forward. Choose what you will focus on next to grow your career and then apply yourself to it with the highest priority.

If you genuinely want to make a difference, then you don't want to produce just for the sake of it. You want to produce quality, and you know intuitively that great work takes time. It doesn't happen overnight while trying to multi-task, or as a result of merely dabbling in the task at hand. Hours of practice occur before a winning performance, weeks of contemplation happen before writing a life-changing program, and years of research is completed before a scientific breakthrough is made.

That is the gift that focused time offers us: the chance to do something extraordinary in our profession, to produce something that has never been seen before, to develop an idea that spreads, and to share something deeply inspiring with the human race. So, even if you have no idea what you will do during your focused time, throw yourself into it anyway.

Switch off the newsfeed, the television, and the drama around you and focus on your future, on developing the skills you need, on achieving the success you seek; whatever it is that is of importance to you. This practice of putting your purpose ahead of the million other things that could consume your valuable energy and creativity will reward you ten-fold.

A friend once had a sign on the wall beside his bedroom door that had three questions on it: where am I going, what am I doing, and why am I doing it? Every time he left the house, they prompted him to reassess how he was about to invest the next 24 hours. Would it help or hinder him? Was he moving in the direction he wanted to go? Or was he ignoring his intuition that was prompting him not to do what he was planning to do?

These three simple yet powerful questions reminded him that how he spent his minutes either contributed to or distracted him from achieving his goals, which included the people he spent his time with. Your time is the container within which your entire life happens. That is why, if you don't learn to concentrate and channel your time and you dissipate and waste it instead, you will spin your wheels while others are getting ahead. Consequently, you will miss out on the life that is possible for you.

Directing your time towards the fulfilment of your purpose might mean pushing back on your commitments, reassessing relationships, releasing responsibilities, and even wrapping up projects and jobs that are using too much of your most precious resource. But I can guarantee you this: the world will not stop spinning and your world will not fall apart if you change what you devote your time to.

In fact, your fears about what you think could or will happen when you decide to spend the first hour of your day reading, allocate time for the most important tasks, or schedule regular personal reflection into your calendar may be completely unfounded.

Making one change at a time and communicating clearly with the people around you will be your go-to strategies for transforming your life by improving your time management. Start small by declining invitations to events that don't inspire you and work your way up from there. Be clear on what you are doing, when, and why, and inform the people that need to know about it.

As a general rule, people are far more independent and resourceful than you might think. They don't need you 24 hours a day, and with the right system in place, even your business can run smoothly without you being all 'hands on deck', seven days a week. You don't have to respond to everyone and everything that happens. In most cases, this is a fast-track to a whole lot of motion without any traction.

You will always have a to-do list. There will always be things you haven't done and things you need to organise. There will forever be people who need or want things from you. You will never get it all done, finish your work completely, or have everything in tip-top shape. It's impossible; that is just a part of life.

What matters is whether you are making time for your soul's work. Whether you are putting what matters ahead of that which doesn't. Whether you are willing to let go of trivial pursuits and get on with the pursuit of your lifetime - your purpose. Whether you are moving forward on the projects and plans that have deep and lasting meaning for you... whether you are doing what you were born to do. That is what counts.

Your time is limited and precious, and the greatest pain you will ever feel is the pain of wasting your life on irrelevancy. As Benjamin

Franklin said, "If we take care of the minutes, the years will take care of themselves." So, are you prioritising your calling? Making time for what inspires you? Doing what moves you from within? Or are you giving your time away? Listen to the messages from your beating heart; they know the way. Prioritise the mission that you yearn to fulfil and the great things you feel born to do.

Leave Your Legacy for Humanity

The conversation about leaving a legacy for humanity is a conversation about the difference that you can make in this world by being exactly who you are. It is a conversation about the unique impact you can have on the human race by pursuing your calling religiously, every single day.

It is a conversation about the work you can do by being willing to make your life about something far more meaningful than what happens on a day-to-day basis - a vision so inspiring that it brings tears to your eyes. It is a conversation about what only you can do with your God-given gifts and talents. And, it is a conversation about the contribution that only you can make by following your inspiration wherever it takes you.

The moment when you realise that you have something inside you that can help another human being is a significant one. When you discover that you are not just here, but that you are here for a purpose grander than anything you have ever imagined before, life will never be the same again. It can be a profound turning point in your journey; the spark of a radically different future, a change to a career that lights you up from within, and a whole new lease on life.

All the wondering about whether it all adds up in the end will be over. No longer will you have to worry about what you will do with the rest of your life, because you will finally know. The mystery will be solved, and you will be able to get busy building your dream.

I remember that moment in my journey as if it was yesterday; when I realised that my love of writing didn't have to end with me and that I could, in fact, design my entire life around it. That was the same day I found the confidence I'd been searching for as well as what turned out to be the greatest roadmap to my dreams. It happened in the same year I discovered my purpose as an inspirational writer.

You may recall that I began writing poetry and short prose in my early teenage years. Within a few months, I had compiled a selection of my writings and titled it *December's Child* (now you know which month I was born in). I printed and bound 40 copies and gifted them to my teachers and fellow students. A week later, one of my girlfriends said to me, "I read this at night, and it helps me to work through my feelings." That was the moment I got it: when 14-year-old Emily realised that she had something inside her that she could share with people.

That moment, when it happens for you, is where your legacy is born. It is the acorn for your oak tree, and once you find that acorn, all that will be left for you to decide is how many people you want to touch, how far you want your ripple to reach, and where you want your own life to go in the process.

There is no written rule that says you can't be one of the great legends that walks the planet, someone who blazes a trail with their presence and their work. Your life belongs to you and you are the one who ultimately chooses whether, where, how and with who you will share your gifts.

To catch a glimpse of what your legacy might be, ask yourself this: "How will the world know I was here?" Think about what you will do that could touch lives in a significant way. What books will you write for future generations to read? What company might you start that provides services, products, and jobs for people? What research will you complete that contributes to breakthroughs in science, technology, or medicine? What art, performances, or works could you create to captivate people? What will you leave behind you in the world?

Leaving a legacy does not mean that you have to revolutionise a government system, build an international corporation, or change the way the world works (unless this is what you are driven to do). Your legacy might be to share your music with people, become the founder of a school that encourages the genius within children, produce breathtaking art or photography, or encourage people to achieve their goals as a coach.

It might be to express yourself on paper, share ancient principles, teach wisdom, cook exquisite food, draw, paint, dance, or show people the beauty of life. Whatever the expression, it just matters that it comes from the depths of what you care about.

You may not be able to comprehend just how significant the impact you can have on humanity can be once you let out what is inside your heart. But the way to find out just how far your influence can reach is to do it; to put yourself out there and offer what you can do to the world.

If this means starting a business, harness the courage to do it, even if you feel afraid at first. If it means reinventing your career or changing industries completely, honour the nudge from within you, even if your next move seems illogical to the people around you. Or, if that means sharing your gifts and abilities with strangers, take a leap of faith and do it, because it is the doorway to the most meaningful career and life you can have.

Imagine what you could do if you dedicated the remaining years of your life to what your soul came to Earth to do. Imagine what might happen if you became devoted to being who you feel you can be and the work that lives inside your heart. What ripple could you send out across the planet? How could your actions and words reverberate through the generations? It could be life-changing for millions.

There will come one or many moments when you realise just how important it is that you pursue your soul's calling and the legacy you know you were born to leave. One of those moments occurred for me while I was writing this very book. It was 8:00 a.m. on a Friday morning and I was about to go to a local café and address my emails for the day.

As I walked there, I received a message from my father's partner telling me that he had been taken to hospital after not being able to move his left arm or shoulder. She didn't know what had gone wrong, but she did know that it was serious enough to contact me.

The news stopped me in my tracks. In a split second, the emails and administration I had been about to take care of were pushed to the back of my mind: I had to go and be with my dad. I dropped everything and travelled two and a half hours to see him in hospital. I didn't notify my team or clients that I was going. I just left. Nothing else mattered more than being there for him. I sat with my dad in the hospital that evening and the following morning, as he started a long journey of recovery from the six ischemic strokes he had experienced in the right hemisphere of his brain.

Despite him being extremely fortunate that the impact of the stroke extended only to his left arm and shoulder, it broke my heart to watch him struggle to do tasks that just two days earlier had come easily to him. Like me, his greatest strength isn't in being patient with himself, and so I sat with him and prayed that he would find the tenderness from within that he needed to make a full recovery, mentally, physically, and emotionally.

The experience impacted me deeply and continues to affect me today. I kept asking myself: what was I working for? What was I trying to accomplish? How did I really want to live? Was I spending my time on what truly counted? Sitting with my dad in a time of adversity showed me how important it is not to work for the sake of working, but to work with cause, purpose, and heartfelt devotion.

It slowed me down from running at a frantic pace so that I could do things consciously with the full force of my love. It reminded me not to waste a single ounce of energy on something that is void of meaning, relationships included. And it reminded me of why I am here - to inspire people - and to let go of everything else.

It is time to do the same for yourself: to remember why you are here and what will matter the most to you when you reach the end of your time on Earth. To remember why you first started out in your field, career, or business. To remember how alive and present you are when doing what you love. To reconnect with the deep purpose of your life.

If you are courageous enough to be devoted to leaving your legacy every single day, then there will come a time when your wildest dreams will come true. So, live every day in pursuit of your greatness. Give yourself wholeheartedly to the future that you dream of. Surrender to your calling and let it lead you towards your ultimate life. Live boldly and without regret. Leave your footprints in the sand and light up the path for others to follow.

And finally, make a commitment to yourself that you will never stop composing your symphony for as long as you live. Why? Because to succeed in extraordinary proportions, by doing what is inside your heart, truly is the greatest gift you can give to yourself and the human race.

*****

As Anais Nin wrote so beautifully, "And the day came when the risk to remain tight in a bud was more painful than the risk it took to blossom." Now is your moment to do exactly this: blossom. There is no time better than now to decide that you will do whatever it takes to live a life full of deep meaning and meaningful accomplishment.

Fortune favours the brave - those who connect with their dream and follow it to the ends of the Earth. That is why it is only in pushing aside trivial dramas and worries and taking a leap of faith every day that you will make your future what it can be. It is only there and then that you will discover that life does have great things in store for you. It is only there and then that you will fulfil your greatest destiny by becoming who you were born to be.

Conclusion

"What lies behind us and what lies before us are tiny matters compared to what lies within us."

Ralph Waldo Emerson

I truly believe that the purpose of life on Earth is to make our time here extraordinary. We weren't put here to suffer, and the trials we encounter, the relationships we experience, the high days and low days, and the whispers from deep inside our heart are all part of the greater plan to have us find our path and flourish. It's just that most people miss the cues, ignore the nudges from their soul, or never give themselves permission to thrive.

Instead, they go through life struggling and settling for less than their heart desires. They feel beaten down by the challenges they face, take things personally, and end up feeling weighed down by regrets about all that they didn't do and didn't pursue. But life doesn't give up on us, not even for one second from the moment we take our first breath to the moment we draw our last.

It is there, 24 hours a day, guiding us to discover and express who we were born to be. It keeps inviting us to follow our heart so that we can make our original mark on the world. It opens windows when doors close and it shows us hope a split second before we are about to give up.

It helps us to become wiser, stronger, and smarter so that we can rise to the occasion when we are called to. It supports us when we are weak and teaches us to fight for what we want against all odds. It shows us that we are wrong when we decide that we have failed or that we don't matter. And when it feels like our world has come to an end, it shows us that it truly is just the beginning. It wants us to be who we were born to be and live the life that we deserve, which is exactly what I want for you.

Maybe the difference between where you are today and where you want to be is so big that it overwhelms you. Maybe you have no idea where to start or you are wondering if your dreams are even possible. And perhaps you will need to make a series of grand gestures and drastic decisions to change your life, be who you want to be, and go where you want to go. It won't always be easy, but the alternative is far tougher: a life where you feel empty inside because you gave up on yourself and your dreams.

It has been my heartfelt wish in writing this book, that you would connect with the greatness inside you and be your brilliant self in the world. I know that you have what it takes to do this, and nothing you can tell me about what has happened in the past or why you think you should throw in the towel can convince me otherwise.

I know that the force that created you, animated you, and shaped you has a bigger plan for you. It doesn't ever lose sight of the vision of what can happen once you become ignited from within. It believes in you the same way I do. It knows you have the potential to rise again after facing great adversity and that you can go to great places.

We are all on a journey; part of one big family experiencing what it is to be human. We are all vulnerable at times and we are all learning and growing. We can't predict what will happen tomorrow. Only heaven knows how our fate will pan out, but we can steer our life in the direction we choose, and once you catch a glimpse of your inspiring vision for the future, you will no longer settle for a life that passes as satisfactory.

Instead, you will want to make the absolute most of your time by experiencing the immense rewards, meaningful blessings, and unconditional love that is available to each and every one of us. Every single day adds up to the whole, and so how you live today - this day, right here and right now – is what defines the journey you will take.

So, no matter what happens, don't ever forget you were born with a higher purpose in mind - the divine inspiration for your existence - and that the real meaning and magic of your life is found and felt when you fulfil that purpose. It is when you do this that you will connect with your greatness and spiral upwards towards your destiny.

From this place, you can set the world alight with your brilliance, inspire it with your talents, help it with your gifts, and warm it with the love inside your heart. You can inspire others to unleash their greatness, too. You came to Earth to do something deeply inspiring, for both yourself and for humanity. So, realise it, do it, and persist with it.

I wrote *Born Great* to make sure that you share who you are with humanity, so that we don't miss out on the gifts you have to offer. I have poured my heart into every page of this book in an attempt to encourage you on the path towards your dreams and give you every confirmation you will ever need that great things await you if you have the courage to be yourself and pursue your purpose relentlessly.

It is my hope that you have discovered this, and so much more, and that you are ready to take your life into your own hands and mould it to your heart's content. And it is my wish that, from this day forward, you will devote yourself to living an extraordinary life and that you won't let anything knock you off that path.

You are far more capable, brilliant, inspiring, and extraordinary than you know, and you were born for greater things. The fact that this book has found its way into your life is proof of that. So, take each step confidently and with your whole heart. Have faith in the greater plan for you and follow your inspiration wherever it takes you.

Lean into life and know that it will be there if you fall. Embrace your challenges as an opportunity to excel, stand out, and shine, and don't let anything stop you from bringing your heartfelt dream to life. Go forth and make an incredible mark on the world because you truly were BORN GREAT.

You Were Born Great

"You were born for more.

Born to do more than you are today.

Born to be more than you are today.

Born to shine brighter - more light.

Born to be higher than you are - more altitude.

You were born to rock, roll, and rise.

You were born with a grand purpose in mind.

God and life have a plan for you.

YOU are the plan, walking on Earth.

Living, walking, breathing, feeling, thinking.

Evolving, pulsing, changing, morphing.

You were born to follow the plan.

Your entire life guides you to it.

Your challenges make you wiser for it.

Your sadness makes you richer for it.

Your heart is filled with love for it.

Your soul guides you to it.

You were born for more.

You were born to speak the voice in you.

Born to stand for the cause that moves you.

Born to fulfil upon your grandest callings.

Born to break through any limits before you.

Born to be wise, smart, beautiful, graceful, tall.

This world needs your gifts, talents, and skills.

It has holes that only you can see and complete.

It has problems that only you can solve.

God patiently waits for us to fulfil our visions.

For us to stand in our giftedness.

For us to SEE what the universe sees in us.

Our pure, potent light and love and potential.

For us to DO what the universe knows we can do.

Travel to great horizons and transform ourselves in the pursuit of all that matters to us.

For us to KNOW all that we truly are as human beings.

Brilliant. Awe-inspiring. Inspirational to those around us.

For us to FEEL what it wants us to feel.

That we were born for a destiny.

Born for a cause.

Born for a reason.

Born for more."

Emily Gowor

Acknowledgements

Firstly, my appreciation goes to Cal Newport for igniting my original inspiration for this book. It was while reading Cal's profound book, *Deep Work*, that the idea for *Born Great* first came to me. Within four short weeks, I had written nearly 40,000 words of what I felt would be my most inspired work yet.

Thank you from the depths of my heart to Philip Krieg for seeing my potential and for asking the question that set my entire career in motion. May you rest in peace. Thank you to Laraib Malik for encouraging me to write this book. I am grateful that you have been by my side every step of the way. I love you.

I would love to express my gratitude to Chris Teasdale for standing by me as I brought my masterpiece to life. Thank you also to my author assistant and mother, Rae Antony, for her endless devotion in helping me plan, write, and review this book. To say that your ongoing support and willingness to be my sounding board has been invaluable to me on this journey truly is an understatement. I couldn't have done it without you.

Thank you to Clarissa Judd for teaching me invaluable wisdom about the power of inspired writing at the start of my career. My gratitude extends to Shane Breslin for his contribution to the book; thank you for being an example of the courage to be authentic.

Acknowledgements

Thank you to Tristan for allowing me to mention you as an example of what devotion to one's dream looks like. Thank you also to the wonderful staff at Long Island Campos in Newstead and Market Organics in Newmarket for their warmth, care, and hospitality during my long hours in their cafés writing *Born Great*.

Thank you to the many loved ones who supported me to achieve my goal, including Dr Marcia Becherel, Dr Olivier Becherel, Wayne Mandic, Anthony Hudson, Lisa Burling, Dr Kim Jobst, Dene Martinez, Geoff Alexander, Kim Guthrie, and Sam Poyser. I wish to thank those who inspire me to unleash my greatness, including Dr John Demartini, Ryan Holiday, and Mike Michalowicz. You remind me of what is possible and encourage me to reach for it.

I share my heart with Leo Rodriguez for bringing me much-needed inspiration in the final months of writing the manuscript. My gratitude extends to the team who assisted me in the production and publishing of this book and to Maryono for the book cover design; thank you for working with me to bring my vision to life. And finally, thank you to my readers. You are the reason I write. I believe in you.

About The Author

Emily Gowor is an inspirational writer, author, and speaker.

After overcoming depression at age 19, Emily devoted herself and her life to bringing writing and inspiration to the world. She has now spent more than a decade showing people that it is possible to live an extraordinary life.

As the author of more than ten published books on the topics of self-help, entrepreneurship, and writing, Emily produced an award-winning blog, *Life Travels*, in 2010 and 2011.

Emily's writings and speaking presentations have touched and moved thousands globally as she inspires people to reach for more. As a winner of the 2012 and 2014 Anthill 30under30 Young Entrepreneur Award, Emily has been featured in a range of media sharing her inspirational messages.

Having fulfilled upon a profound and thriving career in her twenties, Emily finds endless inspiration in the world and continues to bring her love for humanity to the forefront into all she does.

For keynote speaking and inquiries, visit:

www.emilygowor.com

www.ingramcontent.com/pod-product-compliance
Ingram Content Group UK Ltd.
Pitfield, Milton Keynes, MK11 3LW, UK
UKHW041438190426
11946UKWH00030B/152/J